Praise for *Decriminalizing Mental Illness: A Practical Model for Building Sustainable Crisis Intervention Teams*

The focus of *Decriminalizing Mental Illness* is collaboration between law enforcement officers and mental health practitioners. However, the book goes above and beyond by providing a forward-looking, much needed matrix model of collaboration between municipal services to maximize efficiency and effectiveness. It gives a step-by-step example of how to build a sustainable public service program in amazing and appreciated yet simple detail.

– Chief Brian Johnson, El Centro Police Department, CA

Decriminalizing Mental Illness is unique and eminently useful! It helps us do what its title promises—and provides bonuses. It organizes the delivery of public services to enhance collaboration between the various agencies and explains how to build capacity for sustaining those services. It gives all of us who serve the public a manual for more effective governance.

– Dick Sears, Mayor, Holly Springs, NC

Decriminalizing Mental Illness reexamines the way we deliver public services. It's a frank and detailed explanation of how to take good ideas from conception to self-sustaining effectiveness. Imagine a practical, proven, research-based checklist of effective practices. You now have it!

– Retired Sheriff Ted G. Kamatchus (U.S. Marshal Southern District of IA)

This book is innovative, inspirational, motivational, and above all, practical. It overflows with the best ideas gleaned from successful Crisis Intervention Team programs and the people who make them work. Keep this reference on your desk. I assure you it will become dog-eared and plastered with notes of your discoveries and insights.

– Thor Eells, Executive Director, National Tactical Officers Association

We're experiencing an epidemic of mental illness in our country. Through fifty years of neglect, we now have a dysfunctional system that criminalizes mental illness rather than one that provides treatment and care. Our broken system has placed a heavy burden on our country's first responders to provide answers for those in crisis with mental health needs. Unfortunately, the answer has often been jail. Now we have a smart new answer for how to address this situation.

Decriminalizing Mental Illness is a new, insightful look at how we build a Crisis Intervention Team (CIT) program that works and lasts!

The MIRACLE system enables first responders to safely handle the immediate concerns and needs of those with mental illness. MIRACLE, collaborating with the National Tactical Officers Association (NTOA) and the National Command & Staff College (NCSC), provides a long-term solution to this crisis. The greatest share of mental health sufferers don't need to be in our jails. They need to be in our communities, living as productively as possible.

Communities can take the CIT Capacity Building process of effective practices and action items to start a program from scratch or improve an existing one and *make their program work.*

Decriminalizing Mental Illness is the answer to how *any* community can begin or strengthen its CIT program, adjusting the process to that community's needs in its own way, for its unique and diverse neighborhoods. Now we have the tactics and strategy to attack this crisis head on.

We have been waiting for this book for a long time!

K. Thor Eells
Executive Director
National Tactical Officers Association
www.newwavepublishers.com/cit

Decriminalizing Mental Illness is brilliant. It covers so much more than decriminalizing mental illness through collaboration between law enforcement and mental health agencies. Imagine untangling the web of delivering any local public service by explaining it in terms of a program's life cycle. How simple, how elegant, how doable. A single reading will boost your chances of building a successful program many times over.

– Chief Randy Watt, Ogden Police Department, UT

Finally, a book that focuses on Crisis Intervention Team (CIT) training. We know it's not just training, and this book sets forth a way in which cities and towns can solve the problems they face through a new approach: By decriminalizing mental illness, they protect the safety of their staff, their citizens, and their communities. Getting people to treatment, not to jail, is the answer. And this can be applied to all public sector programs, using this book as a roadmap. You will put this book to work.

– Deby Dihoff, Executive Director, NAMI, NC

This book maps the future for delivering public services. Cities and towns can solve their problems, no matter how intractable the issues may seem. Building the foundational capacity of resources to deliver a service is the sensible answer—and now we have a roadmap to do so. *Decriminalizing Mental Illness* provides an example of how this approach can work for all public sector programs. Bravo!

– Sheriff Dave Mahoney, Dane County Sheriff's Office, WI

Capacity Building Series: Volume II
Second Edition

Decriminalizing Mental Illness

A Practical Model for Building Sustainable Crisis Intervention Teams

Books in Capacity Building Series

Volume I. *Building Capacity from the Bottom Up: The Key to Sustaining Local Services*

Volume II. *Decriminalizing Mental Illness: A Practical Model for Building Sustainable Crisis Intervention Teams,* 2nd Ed.

Volume III. *Accelerating Juvenile Reentry: A Practical Capacity Building Model for Sustaining Aftercare*

Volume IV. *Accelerating Adult Reentry: A Practical Capacity Building Model for Sustaining Post-Release Transitional Services*

Capacity Building Series: Volume II
Second Edition

Decriminalizing Mental Illness

A Practical Model for Building Sustainable Crisis Intervention Teams

James Klopovic
with
Nicole Klopovic

Decriminalizing Mental Illness: A Practical Model for Building Sustainable Crisis Intervention Teams

Published in the United States by Affinitas Publishing

Except as noted, the web addresses referenced in this book were live and correct at the time of the book's publication but may be subject to change.

Editing: Peggy Henrikson, Heart and Soul Editing
Cover and interior design: Nick Zelinger, NZ Graphics
Virtual Assistance: Kelly Johnson, Cornerstone Virtual Assistance, LLC
Indexing: Sandi Schroeder, Schroeder Indexing

Publisher's Cataloging-in-Publication
(Provided by Cassidy Cataloguing Services, Inc.)

Names: Klopovic, James, author. | Klopovic, Nicole, author.

Title: Decriminalizing mental illness : a practical model for building sustainable crisis intervention teams / James Klopovic, with Nicole Klopovic.

Description: Second edition. | [Morrisville, North Carolina] : Affinitas Publishing, [2025] | Series: Capacity building series ; volume 2 | Includes bibliographical references.

Identifiers: ISBN: 978-0-9982372-8-2 (softcover) | LCCN: 2024925750

Subjects: LCSH: Crisis intervention (Mental health services)--Planning. | Community mental health personnel--Training of. | Mentally ill offenders--Services for. | People with mental disabilities and crime. | Organizational effectiveness.

Classification: LCC: RC480.6 .K56 2025 | DDC: 362.204251--dc23

10 9 8 7 6 5 4 3 2 1

2nd Edition

Printed in the United States of America.

DEDICATION

Doug, Bobby, and Anson, you still inspire.

If you want to go fast—go alone.
If you want to go far—go together.

– African Proverb

Acknowledgments

Acknowledging all the individuals who contributed to this book in some way would be impossible, so a heartfelt thank you goes out to everyone collectively. Be-yond those who helped with the book's content and publication, we owe a great debt to all who devote time and effort to building and participating in community service programs that improve the common good.

Pursuing a local strategy of decriminalization and reentry of people who live with mental illness is bold, even audacious. Success rides on the multiple collaborations involved. The intent is noble, and the results improve and may even save many lives. These dedicated people deserve heartfelt recognition for helping to change the world *one person at a time.*

This book is the work of years and represents the contribution of many wonderful people. They shared their thoughtful reflections and often endured days of inquiry about what they do and know. Without their input, support, and especially encouragement, this book would not exist.

Much gratitude goes to Gerry Akland, Bonnie Currie, Deby Dihoff, Crystal Farrow, Chris Flannigan, Christopher "Chris" M. Hoina, Sr., Terry Ingram, Ann Oshel, Chris Wassmuth, and Sergeant Kim Wrenn.

Many thanks also to Team Affinitas: Editor Peggy Henrikson is the Gandalf of editing and a dear friend. I am a writer; she makes me an author. Virtual Assistant Kelly Johnson is a true IT wizard and one who brings cheer to every day. Designer Nick Zelinger is award winning and nationally renowned and respected. These three, along with Indexer Sandi Schroeder, provided their publishing expertise to enhance the quality of this book.

Finally, I can't give acknowledgments without mentioning my daughters, Cindy and Nicole, who are in my heart every day, even when we are far apart. Nicole is the cofounder and CEO of The Nicole and James Klopovic Family Charitable Foundation, which we formed to support public programs that do good in the world. This Capacity Building Series will be its operating manuals. The Foundation and Nicole are the reasons I write.

Thank you all. James Klopovic

A Note About Artificial Intelligence

We encourage you to use this remarkable tool to enhance your idea as you build your program's capacity. However, it must augment planning, operation, and sustainability. This book on Capacity Building represents years of work studying and documenting how outstanding people have made decriminalizing mental illness with crisis intervention teams *work well in practice.*

Therefore, yes, take advantage of AI, but keep in mind the following: AI *does not and cannot* substitute for the extensive "street view"—even "worm's-eye" view—research covering what works in building this practical, proven model. AI cannot assess the local politics, personalities, processes, and procedures you will use to turn your good idea into a working, sustained program.

Secondly, and most importantly, AI can give you the sense of moving forward while hindering your progress. As a planner, you can get *stuck in analysis* with the *feeling* of moving forward. In the end, you must *act* to see what works for you, in *your* community, with *your* idea.

We wish you the best.

James Klopovic and Nicole Klopovic

Contents

LIST OF FIGURES

Preface

I began thinking about Capacity Building in the early 1990s. After retiring from the U.S. Air Force in 1987, I joined the North Carolina Governor's Crime Commission (GCC) for a second career. Somehow, I was assigned to the Analysis Section that evaluated grants. It was light-years away from what shaped me growing up on a farm and two decades with the military. The GCC is the pass-through agency for federal grant funds, which are filtered through the governor to North Carolina's 100 counties and more. Every state has such an entity. Over time, billions are distributed throughout the country, a collective, massive, continuous stream of tax dollars. There is much room for improvement; a great deal is at stake.

Throughout my 25 years at the Commission, I observed and participated in the granting of millions of dollars in thousands of grants just for North Carolina. We managed well over 400-500 grants each year. The GCC processes more now, I'm sure. One year, one major committee of four received just over $70,000,000. All that money could have been spent much more effectively. . . . But how?

I noticed that some grantees "got it." They significantly changed their communities for the better and continued to do so. Others, not so much. I began to study what does and especially what doesn't work. Thank goodness enough goes right to be instructive, even illuminating. Their lessons learned had to be organized, told, and retold. I began to see that nearly *all* grantees never critically looked at the potential they'd have if they concentrated on building their idea to *last* from conception. They needed to evolve past the chaos and rapidity of continually implementing and not achieving permanency. Out of this musing, Capacity Building was born. Old ideas demanded novel rethinking, top to bottom and back again.

As I began my research on the topic, I visited the site of a highly successful juvenile aftercare, where I announced my intention to organize and explain how to do aftercare. The executive director, with the steely-eyed sternness and resigned but resolute voice of years of experience declaimed, "You can't understand, let alone organize, this thing we do. It's all chaos." Thus, he threw the gauntlet.

It wasn't far from the truth to say folks came to work, waited for the first thing to go wrong, then hustled to plug the dike with a longing eye to five o'clock. It was crisis management in action. So much time and potential wasted. Still, many local service projects made their ideas work out of sheer passion, brains, and intestinal fortitude.

But largely, grant-funded projects lived for the next grant—*if* it came. It was a plan to fade away or fail outright. Success was achieved mostly by chance, a lot of work, and a little magic. Staff didn't know how to remove themselves from the chaotic crisis cycle of immediacy, which came at the expense of looking beyond it to permanency. More importantly, it prevented them from creating a success template for the next project—paying it forward.

Figuratively, I picked up the gauntlet. What now, thought I!? Capacity Building demanded an overhaul of the current approach, which began as a list of good things to do to deliver local public services—77 of them to be exact. However, all of these "good things" were an incomprehensible jumble that defied systematic organization and thus meaningful implementation. The order had no rhyme or reason.

Then it dawned on me that everything has a beginning, middle, and end—a Life Cycle. With this concept, chaos becomes a linear process. It bows to true planning, priorities, evidence, and *order,* increasing the effectiveness of collective talent and will. People could understand a Life Cycle. Better yet, they could apply a calculated sequence of proven practices with an eye to building an idea that lasts as long as the problem it addresses endures—finally to stable permanency. Moreover, stakeholders could muster a matrix of other essential talents and services to the cause of the idea. True synergy is possible where the whole becomes greater than the parts.

By then, I was focused on federal policy analysis and saw the need to do better granting—in fact, *much* better granting. Fortuitously, I pursued a doctorate in Public Policy. The topic was to define an evidence-based process to build *Permanent Solutions to Permanent Problems* at the local level. I demanded of myself to design a dissertation that was practical and would make a material difference in people's well-being, neighborhood by neighborhood. This was where problems and their solutions mingled, waiting for inspiration, sweat, and a *plan.*

Now great rigor came to play in studying how to accomplish govern*ance* (the how) not govern*ment* (the what)—through granting in this case. My goal was to help programs realize better results by doing more effective, sustainable program development. I spent seven years earning a degree devoted to Capacity Building, which took on new meaning and practicality with rigorous investigation.

I saw the sensible wisdom of this new approach called Capacity Building. Although a few programs are currently using it with great success, it's slow to catch on because it challenges the system of top-down government with bottom-up-and-back-again govern*ance.* It's a new way of building lasting public programs that improve our neighborhoods with collaboration between all three levels of government (federal, state, and local), as well as the private and private nonprofit sectors. Capacity Building from the bottom up presents ways to build permanency using selected local services and talent to solve local problems. This collaborative matrix becomes focused and more—much more—than the sum of its parts.

To begin, I needed to define a universal, pervasive, and persistent problem to analyze and for which to suggest solutions. This problem had to be reentry, which is a concern, I can safely say, of *every* community in the country. Tackling it had to involve a community-wide strategy, and it had to start with prevention of the problem in the first place. Thus, it needed to include:

- Keeping our *children* in school and helping them be successful—by far the most successful crime prevention action we can take.
- Helping our *mental health consumers* to stay out of the criminal justice system and remain at home or in the workforce as productive members of their communities.
- Supporting our *troubled youngsters* to get back on the path to self-sufficiency and good citizenship.
- Helping those who run afoul of the criminal justice system to return to respectability and productivity as a part of community.

These steps represent a comprehensive strategy for reentry, township by township. Furthermore, a municipality can begin with only one element of the strategy, depending on their resources and especially their determination to succeed. This model for public services is based on prevention, intervention, and resolution of a universal, intergenerational problem. After all, having *no* reentry strategy is extravagantly expensive in public dollars and individual suffering, which these capacity-built programs could help alleviate. For those willing to address these issues, Capacity Building is the way.

Remember that discussion with the program director who said taming the chaos of services can't be documented? Well, this book is part of a four-volume set documenting just that—taming chaos, bringing order, and permanently solving a universal problem, one project, one community at a time.

This is a major life work for me—and its own reward. As Henry David Thoreau wrote in *Walden,* "If one advances confidently in the direction of his dreams, and endeavors to live the life which he has imagined, he will meet with a success unexpected in common hours." Who knows where these volumes will go and what effect they will have. I do know that whatever happens, it will be good. At least, these volumes in the Capacity Building Series can guide the generations that follow me in building local service ideas that are *Permanent Solutions to Permanent Problems.* If even one effective, lasting program results, it's been worth everything it's taken to realize these volumes and this dream of a lifetime.

– James Klopovic

How to Get the Most Out of This Book

Each volume in the Capacity Building series begins with a checklist of action items and effective practices. It helps you see in a few pages what it takes to build your service idea to permanency.

When your idea becomes permanent by generating its own resources for sustainability, you've been successful. Only permanency will allow you to begin to close your services-to-needs gaps and make permanent, meaningful improvements in your community. Success is critical, as it's tougher to start another idea after a failure.

Note that each volume of the Capacity Building series covers a different aspect of making your community safer. They're similar but not the same. Volume I: *Building Capacity from the Bottom Up: The Key to Sustaining Local Services* explains the Capacity Building model. It also addresses the needs of our youngest citizens to help keep them out of the justice system in the first place. Volumes II through IV address Capacity Building for specific programs: *Decriminalizing Mental Illness, Accelerating Juvenile Reentry, and Accelerating Adult Reentry.* You're encouraged to refer to the Implementation checklists for each volume of Capacity Building, as you'll find a wealth and variety of practical advice that you can apply to your specific plan of action. The checklists provide the sequential processes you'll need to develop your idea and a proven path to success.

The volumes stand alone, yet they overlap and support one another. For each volume, we suggest the following approach:

- *Review* – Review the action-oriented checklist—and think about it.
- *Read* – Study the book, take notes—and think about it.
- *Refer* – Refer to sections in the book that you need as you develop your program.
- *Act* – Go to work, remembering, "Obstacles are only opportunities."

CIT Capacity Building Checklist

The following checklist has been proven successful by your colleagues in the field of decriminalizing mental illness with crisis intervention teams. In the Appendix, you'll find a duplicate of this (Fig. 1-B) as well as other checklists, procedures, and plans to give you a comprehensive head start and guides for the various aspects of your program.

While it's important to hew to the life cycle, action items, and effective practices, we recommend you continuously modify this checklist to fit your needs. Adhering to its basics, however, is a proven way to enhance your chances of success.

Fig. 1-A. CIT Capacity Building Checklist – PHASES I-III, with Key Action Items and Effective Practices
PHASE I of the Project Life Cycle: Plan and Implement
1. Nurture and grow key leadership. Assemble your core group of CIT champions and leaders.
Assemble a core group of change agents responsible for making CIT happen.
State your CIT vision, mission, goals, and values as guides to daily decision making.
Assemble key stakeholders and get buy-in.
Meet regularly in an organized fashion with an emphasis on purpose.
Organize work by functional committees and standardized operations.
2. Develop a strategic plan.
Develop an action-oriented strategic plan.
3. Determine project scope.
Develop project scope by mapping clientele and community resources.
Assess readiness to implement CIT.
Establish a 24/7, no-refusal crisis response.
4. Map local services and create a common playbook.
Map local services that are alternatives to arrest for law enforcement.
5. Design impact analysis.
Understand the costs of arrest to develop an argument for CIT.
Develop essential measurements of decriminalizing individuals with mental illness that appeal to key stakeholders.

6.	**Nurture relationships.**
	Develop relationships to secure resources beyond money.
	Develop marketing strategies
7.	**Develop training to fit both officers and consumers.**
	Design CIT training to fit both law enforcement and the mental health consumer.
8.	**Develop staff for performance and team effort.**
	Choose law enforcement-oriented CIT coordinators.
	Choose performance-oriented CIT class instructors.
	PHASE II: Operate and Stabilize
9.	**Plan operations with the future in mind. Gear leadership for permanency.**
	Establish a CIT advisory board for oversight and necessary work.
	Strengthen the CIT collaborative between law enforcement and mental health CIT coordinators.
	Pilot your first 40-hour CIT class with officers from one sheriff's office.
	Continuously build and rebuild your community-based resources.
	Actively pursue your plan for CIT stability.
	Continuously redefine program scope as the gap between capacity and demand becomes apparent.
	Automate process monitoring (efficiency) and impact analysis (effectiveness) as much as possible.
	Develop and use an array of marketing tools to get the word out.
	Choose law enforcement trainees who want to work with mental health consumers.
	Maintain a core group of mental health services instructors who identify and connect with first responders.
	Have the CIT coordinator be responsible to the lead law enforcement executive.

PHASE III: Sustain and Expand
10. Sustain operations by continuous redefinition.
Redefine scope: Restate vision, mission, and goals.
11. Plot your long-range strategy and tactics for scaling up.
Continue to strengthen the comprehensive jail diversion network.
Assemble a transition team to close the services-to-needs gap.

Now you have an overview of how the elements of Capacity Building fit together for your endeavor. The rest of the book explains each step in detail to answer your questions or lead you to the appropriate answer.

Herein is *wisdom* attained from experience. Visualize the **Life Cycle** of your idea. This makes your vision real.

Herein is *logic.* Build your idea with **Key Actions**—what actions to take when you need to take them. See your project taking shape.

Herein is *purpose.* **Effective Practices** are just that—*effective.* You must act, but not haphazardly without a mission and especially a vision just out of reach to be challenging thus rewarding.

Process matters. Moving relentlessly, productively, with this proven process is the antidote for confusion and failure. The process is *simple* but not simplistic; it's *suitable* for any good local service program.

Mold your program to your local circumstances, politics, and people—and especially to your mix of staff and partners. It will be *yours.* As you progress, add, edit, and refine your path. That way, you're building your implementation plan of action for your *next* idea—or to help *others* make a permanent difference as well.

The aim is to help create communities where people can live, work, play, be content, and *thrive.*

Capacity Building is 21st-century governance. *Lead it.*

CHAPTER PREVIEWS

Chapter 1: Introducing Crisis Intervention Teams (CIT)

Crisis Intervention Teams are the heart of decriminalizing mental illness. This chapter places CIT as a critical element in your overall municipality-wide reentry strategy. It also shows that a successful CIT program is an example of building any local service idea from the bottom up. The CIT operation represents good governance going forward, if only for the funds and effort that are economized, targeted, and successfully employed. Decriminalizing mental illness greatly reduces burdens on local public infrastructure, especially jails and the criminal justice system. Further, this chapter explains how the program is built on applicable matrices of local resources and is scalable to the need. It includes results from stakeholder interviews from successful CIT programs and site visits and demonstrates that Capacity Building works.

Chapter 2: The CIT Capacity Building Model – More Than a Good Idea

This chapter introduces the criticalities for making CIT work. When built with the capacity to endure, the program is dynamic and adaptable. The chapter explains smart things to do in developing CIT, such as seeing progress in terms of a Life Cycle. It also considers what elements motivate participants, the importance of building decision-making data, and especially the limitations of this service idea.

Chapter 3: Phase I. Plan and Implement

Chapter 3 addresses planning, the most essential yet the *least understood and most ignored part* of local services development and delivery. Not attending to planning focused on *sustainability* is a prescription for failure. Many programs die in the implementation stage because leaders and planners didn't consider key elements of successful operation. This chapter explains the criticalities you must take into account and actions you must take.

Chapter 4: Phase II. Operate and Stabilize

Only action will teach you the best way forward and how to stay on track. This chapter explains how to make your daily operations work well and stabilize. It addresses topics such as gearing leadership to permanency, developing collaboration between law enforcement and mental health teams, assessing capacity, evolving scope, automating evaluation and analysis, developing marketing tools, and establishing key staff.

Chapter 5: Phase III. Sustain and Expand

Chapter 5 explains how you must continuously redefine operations as your true needs become apparent. It stresses the importance of plotting long-range strategies and tactics for scaling up and provides wisdom from CIT successes.

Chapter 1

INTRODUCING CRISIS INTERVENTION TEAMS (CIT)

Chapter 1

INTRODUCING CRISIS INTERVENTION TEAMS (CIT)

Durham, Ontario's Crisis Intervention Team combines a psychiatrically trained registered nurse with a CIT officer

"The Crisis Intervention Team (CIT) is a community partnership consisting of law enforcement officers, mental health providers, those living with mental illness, and their family members. [These partners collaborate] to understand mental illness, invest time and effort to avert crises, work to de-escalate crises, and direct the person to appropriate care."
– Gerry Akland, advocate, National Alliance on Mental Illness (NAMI)

One of the most difficult issues facing our communities, our leaders, and the criminal justice system is how to respectfully handle and help those living with mental illness. Far too often, these individuals are treated as criminals and end up incarcerated rather than given the care they need. Most times an arrest is the only alternative. Why? Mainly because the mental health system has not been equipped to handle the need. Also, law enforcement agents haven't been given the training and resources to deal with those living with mental illness. The consequences can be devastating. The community spends more time and money, and the individuals involved and their families incur further distress. Diversion is a simpler and more effective alternative if properly planned, implemented, and sustained.

A Local Reentry Strategy and Crisis Intervention Teams

Reentry in this context refers to returning people who live with mental illness to their communities after a disturbance and after they've been given the requisite care to be productive citizens. It's also about continuing the care and resources the people who struggle need to prevent recidivism. The Crisis Intervention Team (CIT) model proposed here is a critical part of any local reentry strategy. It's important that a strategy be developed locally because this population is better served in and by their own communities, where their families and connections are located.

This book emphasizes that a local CIT program is *an* answer *not the* answer to decriminalizing mental illness. The municipal challenge is how to avoid using the criminal justice system and instead use local resources as an alternative to incarceration. This is one of the most vexing local social conundrums. There is no single answer.

Experience reveals an underuse or misallocation of local resources, which need focus and organization. Proper use and allocation require an overall strategy. First and foremost, we want to keep people out of the criminal justice system in the first place. Then we want to help those involved with the criminal justice system transition back into their communities. Thus, every municipality needs an overarching strategy (as detailed by the Capacity Building Series) to:

- keep children in primary and secondary school,
- decriminalize mental illness,
- accelerate juvenile aftercare, and
- accelerate adult reentry.

The Sequential Intercept Model

Decriminalizing mental illness in itself requires an overarching strategy—beyond building a self-sustaining CIT program. One of the best is the Sequential Intercept Model (SIM). Essentially, SIM is a strategic planning tool that outlines agencies and stakeholders to consider with your long-term CIT Capacity Building process. The following SIM chart is from the Policy Research Associates' SIM Model brochure.[1]

Fig. 2. Sequential Intercept Model

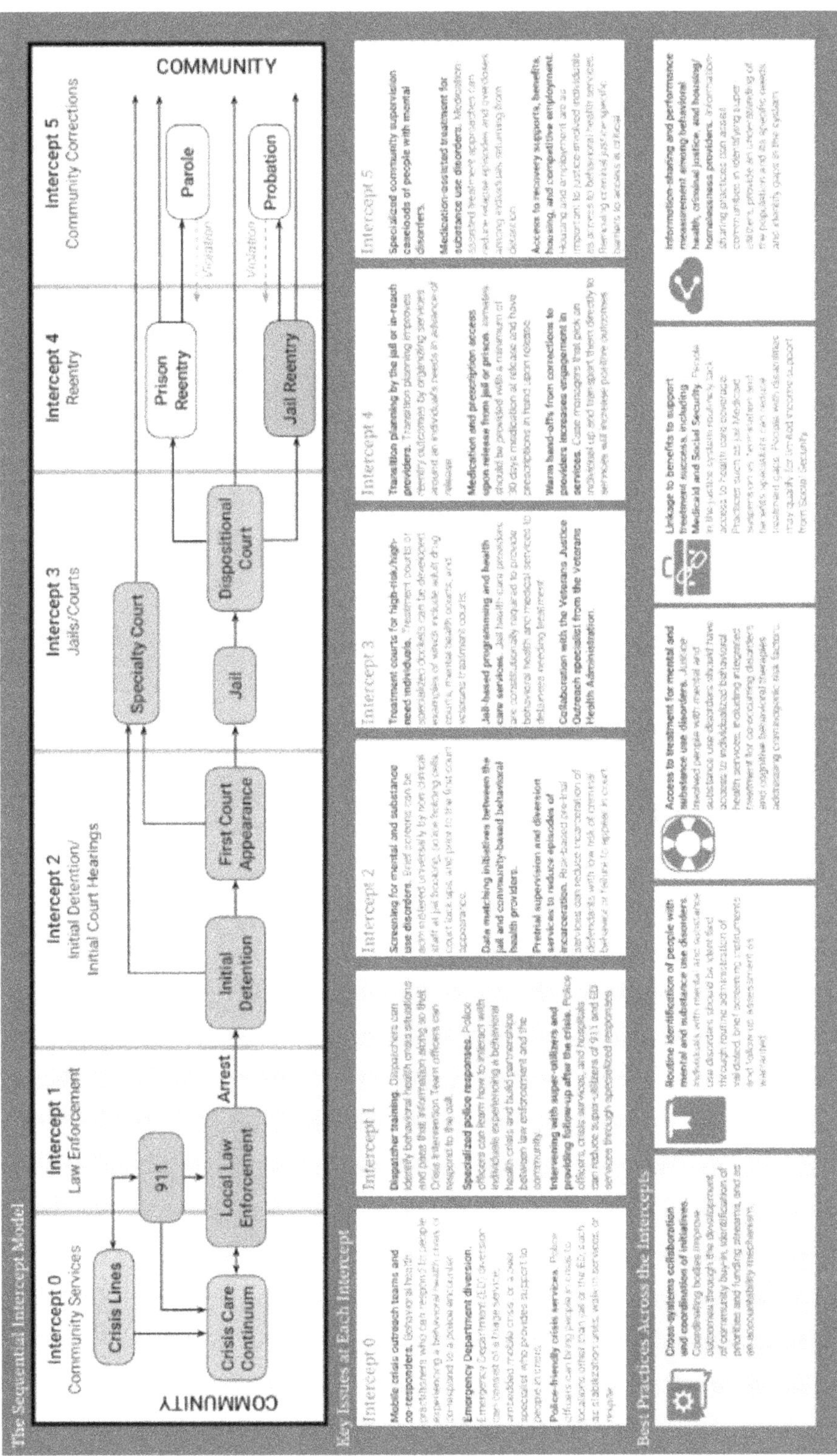

The Sequential Intercept Model is most effective when used as a community strategic planning tool. Use it to assess available resources, determine gaps in services, and plan for community change to decriminalize mental illness. These activities are best accomplished by a team (matrix) of stakeholders that includes multiple systems and agencies. Stakeholders may be from mental health, substance abuse, law enforcement, pretrial services, courts, jails, community corrections, housing, health, social services, people with the experience of mental illness or addiction, family members, and many others.

Employed as a strategic planning tool, communities can use the Sequential Intercept Model to:

1. Develop a comprehensive picture of how people with mental and substance use disorders flow through the criminal justice system along six distinct intercept (decriminalizing) points: (0) Community Services, (1) Law Enforcement, (2) Initial Detention and Initial Court Hearings, (3) Jails and Courts, (4) Reentry, and (5) Community Corrections.
2. Identify gaps, resources, and opportunities at each intercept for adults with mental and substance use disorders.
3. Determine priorities for action to improve system and service-level responses for adults with mental and substance use disorders.

CIT as Part of the Plan

As part of an overall strategy, CIT is realistic and doable. In addition, the long-term benefits in dollars and cents, risk and liability reduction, and community well-being are cumulative and significant.

Crisis Intervention Teams are important for *every* community. They include disparate agencies, law enforcement officials, mental health and service professionals, and advocates for the people who live with mental illness. When implemented properly, a CIT program provides a significant return on investment for multiple reasons. The program:

- *Provides care* – The mentally ill individuals involved (herein also referred to as people living with mental illness, mental health services consumers, mental health consumers, or simply consumers) get the care they need without prolonged involvement with the criminal justice system.

- *Avoids expenses* – Most often the criminal justice system avoids unnecessary expenses when a well-planned and sustained CIT program is in place. Mental health consumers are one of the most expensive populations to incarcerate.
- *Expedites services* – Local public sector agencies can allocate the services and mental health resources consumers need more efficiently and effectively than the criminal justice system.
- *Multiplies efforts* – The community wins by the compounding effect of efforts and cooperation to decriminalize its population.
- *Benefits citizens* – Equally important, citizens win for all these reasons and by having consumers served much more appropriately than being arrested.
- *Allocates resources* – Limited financial and especially human resources are much more efficiently and effectively allocated than without such a program.
- *Reduces harm* – When a consumer is properly handled, use of force is reduced, and all concerned, especially the family, have a happier ending to the incident.

Contributing to a CIT program is one of the best ways to become involved in community betterment and well-being. If you accept the challenge of committing to the Capacity Building format and philosophy, you will serve your community well. You will become more of who you are in the highest sense. In so doing, you will lift those around you, garner respect, experience satisfaction, and leave a legacy of service. Everyone wins.

Implementation and the Reason for the CIT Model

Although the advantages of CIT programs can't be denied, like many other local service ideas, they're difficult to implement. Many programs die at implementation and thus fail to reach their objectives, even though they may have started with great ideas and enthusiasm. That's where this Capacity Building model becomes invaluable. It's a new and proven way to take an idea from conception to stability and, finally, sustainability. Only a self-sustaining program has the backing of communal will and the capacity to continuously address the knotty problem of decriminalizing people living with mental illness.

The Capacity Building Model lays out in detail how successful CIT practitioners have resolved the difficulties of planning, implementation, and operation. It also explains how practitioners have built the necessary support systems for key program phases, milestones, and activities.

Capacity Building

Planning for implementation is a process of Capacity Building because it builds foundational functions. For example, it plans for essential leadership, staffing, resources development, an analysis methodology, and more to help deliver the services. This is done with permanency in mind. It answers the number one reason for the failure of services idea development, which is lack of planning for permanency. Only a permanent program can reach its potential to close the services-to-needs gap and begin to make a difference in the community.

Capacity Building is the business of supporting the services offered. Why is this important? Many (in fact, most) local efforts struggle to begin, let alone to sustain their service idea. Even if they survive, they rarely reach their potential. What more will be possible if the chaos of beginning a CIT program can be organized and clarified by a proven, practical process that incorporates checklists? The model presented in this book lays out the steps to prepare for putting CIT into action and then taking it to a state of self-renewing permanence.

Only a self-sustaining program has the backing of communal will and the capacity to continuously address the knotty problem of decriminalizing people living with mental illness.

The current literature and practice on how to build capacity for local service ideas describes bits and pieces of program development individually. It doesn't put them all together in a practical sequence. Without a plan for sustainability, programs are an exercise in reinventing the wheel; they continue to struggle and risk a slow demise. Why not start correctly by focusing on building permanence? Research stresses the need for a sequence of phases, milestones, and actions.[2] It also recommends effective practices determined by those managing already successful CIT programs as part of an overall reentry strategy.

CIT is part of the reform movement in which juvenile and adult reentry aftercare models serve as examples, as described in the research.[3] Such programs represent a 21st-century matrix of targeted local services and resources to resolve difficult situations. These matrix solutions recognize that no single agency or public sector can deliver all the services needed and expected by the citizenry. Collaboration on delivery is vital.

A Bottom-Up Approach

CIT Capacity Building is reforming how top-down agency services are delivered. Single-agency "silo" services work for certain functions such as public transportation, but most services need to be multi-agency in form and function. These matrices combine the efforts of public, private, and private nonprofit entities and focus federal, state, and especially local resources on a single issue from the bottom up.

In the top-down approach, single agencies, which may not be local, take a command-and-control approach and determine both issues and solutions. In the bottom-up approach, a combination of local community practitioners and stakeholders define the issues most important to them. They determine *their* solutions, which are most realistic for *their* unique municipal situation. This approach allows for closer monitoring of the program and a wider foundation of focused, functional leadership.

One of the purposes of local Capacity Building is to develop a skilled, dynamic, character-based leadership workforce to help begin and maintain CIT programs nationally.

The model presented in this book lays out the steps to prepare for putting CIT into action and then taking it to a state of self-renewing permanence.

Just as new juvenile and adult aftercare models are strengths based, so is CIT. This means that rather than playing to the weaknesses of the individuals involved, the program enhances their strengths. It recognizes that most people living with mental illness can lead productive lives when given well-timed assistance. The alternative is being arrested and involved in the criminal justice system. This makes many rehabilitation and maintenance choices more difficult and confers the stigma of having a "record."

> This model for creating CIT programs fills in the missing piece of how to correctly construct a viable, long-term program. Capacity Building is a new area of research. It needs to be the approach of every new service idea at the local level because so many ideas fail or represent a mere sliver of their potential. Not only does the usual approach waste time and money but also the opportunity for significant betterment of the wider community. Capacity Building prevents waste of all kinds, especially effort—and it works.

A Brief Economic Case for CIT - Costs and Tradeoffs

Huge amounts of public monies are saved by avoiding law enforcement's typical response to any disruption of community well-being due to lack of alternatives. Even more insidious is the distraction of sworn officers from their policing duties to transfer someone living with mental illness to services out of the vicinity.

The National Alliance on Mental Illness (NAMI) conducted a survey that illuminated *part* of this serious problem of misallocating resources.[4] For simplicity's sake, only sheriff's offices were polled to determine how many man hours were devoted to transferring custody of those with mental illness—often out of the county. Police departments usually handle transfers within the county. According to the North Carolina Sheriff's Association, sheriff's deputies in the state have spent 228,000 hours on this task—all time away from the primary job of ensuring community safety and security. This statistic is even more dramatic when considering that sheriff's offices number only 100 of over 500 law enforcement entities in North Carolina, most of which can be tasked with transporting someone.

One sheriff monetized an average trip of four hours at $218 for salary and mileage alone. He also commented that a four-hour trip was a short one as it's not uncommon for a deputy to assist a consumer in one capacity or another over a period of *five days.*[5]

Besides the calculable personal benefits for those needing mental health services, a study in 2000 summarized positive results from the Memphis CIT program since its founding. It was the first CIT experiment after a tragic consumer crisis in 1987.[6] The study found that the program:

- *Upgrades perceptions* – The stigma and perception of danger attached to mental illness diminish.
- *Improves officer involvement* – Training equips officers to handle calls related to mental illness rather than resorting to an arrest; most times the only alternative.
- *Reduces violence* – Officers learn how to avoid the use of restraints and reduce the use of force with CIT training, which includes de-escalation techniques.
- *Increases safety* – Both officers and citizens incur fewer injuries.
- *Provides more flexibility with charges* – Officers have greater flexibility in the use of misdemeanor charges.

- *Lowers arrest rates* – The program presents alternatives to arrest.
- *Reduces recidivism* – Recidivism rates dramatically decrease by diverting consumers.
- *Relieves the criminal justice system* – Diversion gives significant relief to an overburdened criminal justice system.
- *Lowers incidences of hostage-taking* – The program nearly puts the hostage negotiation team "out of business."

Regarding the medical emergency room, the program:

- *Better prepares medical staff* – Officers' initial report of medical history better prepares doctors and nurses.
- *Improves officer efficiency* – Officers spend less time in the Emergency Room (ER).
- *Increases safety* – Patient violence decreases.
- *Saves time and money and avoids injuries and health crises* – The need for acute hospitalization of consumers diminishes.
- *Improves care* – Healthcare referrals to consumer-appropriate services increase dramatically.

North Carolina's Goal to Scale CIT and Fit It to Reentry

The availability of CIT training for officers doesn't imply the program is fully planned. North Carolina NAMI representatives stated that the goal is to CIT-certify a critical mass (20 percent) of officers statewide to have the needed impact on the state by decriminalizing mental health clients.

The state had approximately 21,143 law enforcement officers in 2014. Based on these statistics, the proportion of all North Carolina law enforcement officers that were CIT certified by January 1, 2015, was more than 33 percent.[7] These included only police and sheriff's officers. Many more sworn officers plus non-sworn personnel work at the state hospitals, universities, port authorities, and other locations. They, too, can benefit from CIT training.

North Carolina's CIT program development and training are some of the most advanced in the country, providing excellent resources for new programs nationwide.

North Carolina serves as an example of CIT's effectiveness and is a measure of what lies ahead. At this writing more than 11,000 sworn officers have CIT training. That's nearly half of all sworn officers.

Certification and Continuous Training Recommended

According to NAMI and CIT practitioners, once an initial cadre has been trained, it would be helpful to offer continuous certification and awareness training for the following:

- *Sworn staff* – Training for sworn staff is unending due to new hiring, job changes, and retirement.
- *Other agencies* – Emergency responders, telecommunicators, certain hospital staff, and decision makers would benefit from CIT certification and continuous training.
- *Anyone with an interest* – Any citizen or employee with a need or interest to know, such as 911 telecommunicators or people who want to be involved in assisting mental health consumers, can benefit from an abbreviated CIT awareness class.
- *Aftercare* – CIT has great potential to reduce incarceration numbers and expenses when strengthened as part of reentry aftercare programs.

Regarding training, consider a wide variety of need-to-know or simply interested people and groups. For example, what about court personnel, judges, lawyers, and guards? Other first responders? The media? You could include shelter staff and elected officials/community leaders who have a vested interest in their citizens and the services available. Even educators who could notice the first signs of mental illness in juveniles may be interested. Don't forget veterans' support groups that deal with PTSD sufferers. And how about the clergy? Those with mental illness often reach out to places of worship for help.

Consider these interest groups in the planning phase for their eventual inclusion. Once CIT is established and has some caché in the community, many people will want in—even if they don't know it yet!

Moving from Silos to Matrices

Currently, finding answers to the problem of incarcerating mental health consumers is plagued by inertia and risk aversion to any new idea. Resolve to act can be energized by changing the focus. Move to assembling a number of local resources for this purpose rather than depending on a single agency's narrow response. The latter is the "silo" approach. Agencies can develop a "thick wall" and become impervious to flexibility. Their silos can reach into the clouds and become out of touch with ground realities. "Silo busting" is one of the major tasks of directing resources where they do the most good the most efficiently.[8] Look to busting your silos into matrices of services and change the focus from doing a *project* to building *processes*. Encourage the agencies or resources to:[9]

- *Coordinate* - Cross boundaries for new ideas and solutions. Look to cross-train people in various specialties and tasks to increase efficiency and effectiveness. This will also develop better, more creative staff.
- *Cooperate* - Have a multi-agency CIT focus in which the whole multiplies talent and resources rather than a silo single-agency focus.
- *Develop capability* - Create CIT-focused solutions that build capacity.
- *Connect* - Blend services to become stronger than the sum.

Busting silos also busts up inertia and the view of separate, monolithic public services to create true mutual *collaboration*. This new approach combines the listed actions to achieve the goal of delivering services for community well-being. Cooperation epitomizes 21st-century matrix solutions.

Experience demonstrates that sometimes isolated local resources aren't used to the degree they could be for want of a means to collaborate. Crisis Intervention Teams can more effectively handle the varied and immediate needs of a consumer in crisis than individual agencies. CIT anticipates mental health needs by building service capacity where it should be—in the community.[10]

Moving from silo services to networked matrices isn't easy. Efforts to run with a service idea can be short-sighted, terminal, and possibly fatal to the work. Developing an idea is much more than simply delivering services. The platform for its delivery must first be in place, and planning for sustainability is most often neglected.

Successful programs are marked by patience and thoroughness from the beginning, with an "obstacles are opportunities" mentality and action orientation. The results are well worth the effort.

Reducing Burden on Jails: Building CIT from the Ground Up

CIT training begins when law enforcement buys in, and only then can jail diversion begin. But according to one CIT coordinator, those diverted are only a small percentage of mental health consumers currently in the criminal justice system who should have been diverted. How practitioners successfully go about decriminalizing people living with mental illness who are in jail because of a minor offense lies in understanding the process of diversion.

Decriminalizing the consumers through a local jail diversion program based on Crisis Intervention Teams is an effective way to: a) bridge service gaps,[11] b) improve community safety and security,[12] and c) reduce expensive jail/prison populations.[13] The problem of starting an effective CIT program lies in the fragmented understanding of the process of building CIT capacity to the point the program is self-sustaining, that is, permanent, by having dependable operational resources.[14]

Arrest vs. Diversion

Refer to the following flowchart, which graphically depicts what happens with an arrest compared to a diversion.[15] Diversion involves one step.

Fig. 3. Events an Individual with Mental Illness May Experience in the Criminal Justice System

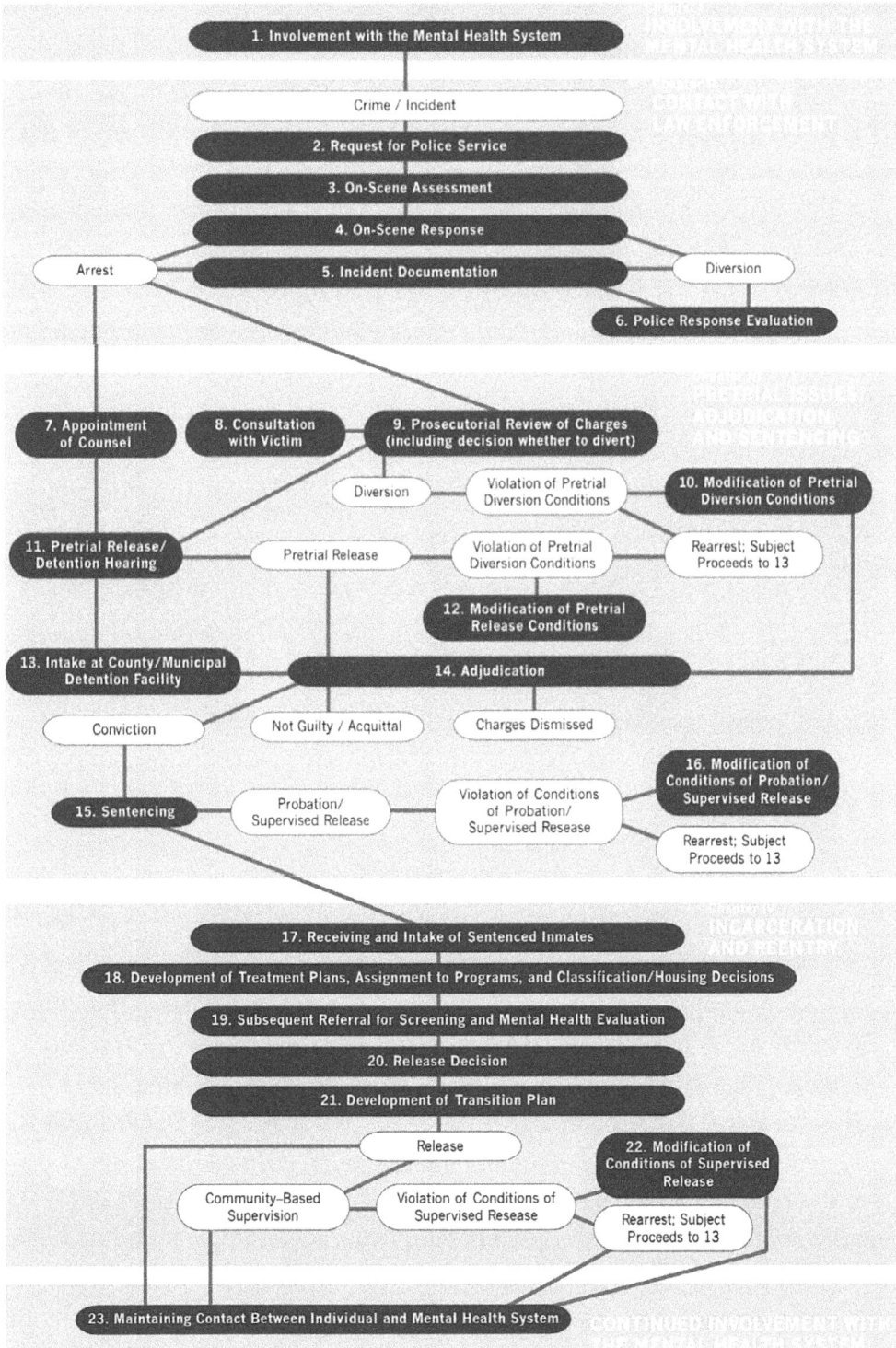

INVOLVEMENT WITH THE MENTAL HEALTH SYSTEM

1. Involvement with the Mental Health System

CONTACT WITH LAW ENFORCEMENT

Crime / Incident

2. Request for Police Service

3. On-Scene Assessment

4. On-Scene Response

Arrest

5. Incident Documentation

Diversion

6. Police Response Evaluation

PRETRIAL ISSUES, ADJUDICATION, AND SENTENCING

7. Appointment of Counsel

8. Consultation with Victim

9. Prosecutorial Review of Charges (including decision whether to divert)

Diversion

Violation of Pretrial Diversion Conditions

10. Modification of Pretrial Diversion Conditions

11. Pretrial Release/ Detention Hearing

Pretrial Release

Violation of Pretrial Diversion Conditions

Rearrest; Subject Proceeds to 13

12. Modification of Pretrial Release Conditions

13. Intake at County/Municipal Detention Facility

14. Adjudication

Conviction

Not Guilty / Acquittal

Charges Dismissed

16. Modification of Conditions of Probation/ Supervised Release

15. Sentencing

Probation/ Supervised Release

Violation of Conditions of Probation/ Supervised Resease

Rearrest; Subject Proceeds to 13

INCARCERATION AND REENTRY

17. Receiving and Intake of Sentenced Inmates

18. Development of Treatment Plans, Assignment to Programs, and Classification/Housing Decisions

19. Subsequent Referral for Screening and Mental Health Evaluation

20. Release Decision

21. Development of Transition Plan

Release

22. Modification of Conditions of Supervised Release

Community-Based Supervision

Violation of Conditions of Supervised Resease

Rearrest; Subject Proceeds to 13

23. Maintaining Contact Between Individual and Mental Health System

CONTINUED INVOLVEMENT WITH THE MENTAL HEALTH SYSTEM

This flowchart depicts the simplicity of diversion and the complexity of arrest. Arrest takes the consumer through as few as two events to as many as 13 separate events to return the individual to the community. Each step is expensive—and this is *before* the expenses of incarceration are incurred.

What the chart does not depict is the wider commitment and work for law enforcement. If charges are pressed, the arresting officer will spend time attending court. Depending on the trial or judgment, the officer may have to return to court several times. This, of course, does not consider how much time an officer spends being with the consumer until another responsible party can assume custody.

A diversion by a CIT trained officer reserves the criminal justice system for those more in need of it, while better allocating scarce resources. Numerous opportunities for diversion exist—before arrest, before booking, before adjudication, and via a mental health court. The earlier the diversion from the institutional response, the better it is for the consumer, the community, and the municipality.

To facilitate understanding of the types of cases CIT confronts, two stories of calls for service follow. First, let's consider Eugene's story.[16]

Diversion Story – Eugene

Three police officers, four firefighters, and two paramedics fill the modest living room. Everyone's attention is focused on Eugene, an agitated 17-year-old who sits on the couch. His grandmother, whose house this is, moves about, volubly retelling her story.

Eugene's grandmother explains that he has just spent 13 days in the Memphis Mental Health Institute (MMHI). CIT officers are trained to change a confrontation into a less hostile meeting. As a starting point, Officer Mike Schafer asks Eugene what medication he is taking. He is told he is taking Haldol (to treat Schizophrenia and other types of psychoses) and Cogentin (to counter the effects of other drugs and help him sleep) for a 30-day trial period. Eugene is to take his medications right before bedtime. This evening, he took them early and then wanted to go out with his friends. His grandmother said he couldn't because he had taken his pills, and an argument ensued.

"He was shouting and perspiring so much he soaked right through his clothes," she said. She had made the 911 call because, in the middle of the altercation, Eugene had suffered chest pains. The paramedics have found nothing physically wrong with him.

CIT Officer Schafer asks Eugene for his version of the events. At times, Eugene seems to lose connection, his eyes rolling. As the crux of the dispute is reached, Eugene jumps up gesticulating and is told firmly to sit back down. He complies and complains about the way the doctor at MMHI looked at him and was reticent about sharing information about his medications. Eugene is desperate for information about his illness.

"I want help," he cries, "but I don't like the medication. I don't feel good. I have chest pains. I need to play basketball so I can get a scholarship to Shelby State. What I want to know is, am I going to be able to run full court if I take the medication?"

Officer Schafer explains that he must take the medication before bedtime, because it will help him sleep. After 30 days his prescription would be reevaluated. As he speaks, he checks with Eugene to make sure he is listening and understands. He also advises Eugene to listen to his grandmother. He lives in her house, and she has his best interests at heart. Back in the patrol car, he shakes his head at the poignancy of Eugene's concerns.

In Eugene's case, the CIT officer's approach avoids arrest. He works to calm the consumer and discover the root of the issue. He assures Eugene that his medications will be reevaluated and advises him to listen to his grandmother, leaving him in her custody. What follows are two very good examples of the flexibility and adaptability of the CIT model as part of reentry.

Memphis, Tennessee

Recognition that people living with mental illness can be decriminalized by bridging services began in Memphis, Tennessee. CIT began formally in 1988, when the Memphis Police Department partnered with the local chapter of NAMI, local universities, and mental health service providers to bridge the gap between services.[17]

Law enforcement was the logical broker of services because sworn officers are typically the first on the scene of a disturbance. Officers have the legally binding mandate to direct a mental services consumer either to jail or to appropriate services.[18] Up until CIT, they had no choice but to "cuff 'em and stuff 'em." An arrest would start a cascade of expensive processes and confer upon the individual the stigma of being a "criminal." With a CIT program in place, simply delivering that consumer to a family member or the appropriate service for needed care avoids all that. So simple to do, yet so difficult to get communities to implement. This book provides a step-by-step procedure for CIT implementation to help alleviate that reluctance. It provides a plan for realistic success in permanently establishing a CIT program to decriminalize many consumers.

The greatest promise in decriminalizing the mentally ill is fulfilled by diverting them from the criminal justice system *before* they become involved in it.[19]

Atlanta, Georgia

With the success of the Memphis model, other states began their own interpretation of jail diversion using trained officers. The centralized model of CIT in Atlanta, Georgia, is another example of adapting CIT to local realities.

Atlanta began somewhat in the dark. Organizers gathered disparate information about program implementation, such as the visioning process and evaluation. They visited Memphis, consulted among themselves, and tackled the difficulties of implementation without a proven, organized way to proceed. They had to learn by potentially repeating mistakes and difficulties other programs had endured. "Reinventing the wheel," they tried to make the Memphis model their own. The route to their current success would have been more direct with a practitioner-based manual explaining how to go about the task.

With the knowledge this book provides, those building new CIT programs can minimize mistakes and greatly reduce the time to implementation. The path to program stability will be more realistic and program sustainability more assured. Then practitioners can begin to incrementally scale to meet demand. Public services rarely reach this state of affairs, but Capacity Building makes stability and growth far more possible and likely.

The greatest promise in decriminalizing the mentally ill is fulfilled by diverting them from the criminal justice system *before* they become involved in it.

The greatest promise in decriminalizing the mentally ill is fulfilled by diverting them from the criminal justice system before they become involved in it.

Let's look at another story of diversion.[20]

Diversion Story – Helena

In an upper middle-class neighborhood, the front door of the house stands wide open. In the kitchen, a 28-year-old woman, Helena, leans languidly against the counter, flanked by two paramedics and faced by a police officer.

Sleepy, depressed, Helena responds slowly and with tonal flatness to Officer Schafer's questions as he establishes the chain of the evening's events. She had been out drinking at a neighborhood bar with her husband. Arriving home, she took a large quantity of her husband's antibiotics, Cephalexin, washed down with vodka. The nearly empty bottle stands on the counter. Initially, her husband had no idea his wife was in distress, and he is still off balance. It is he who called 911. One of the other officers takes him to another room to ask about his version of events and allow Helena the privacy to speak her mind.

Officer Schafer asks Helena why she took the pills. She replies, "I'm tired of life. Life is so heavy."

"Did something happen between you and your husband?"

Helena shakes her head as Officer Schafer explains that she will have to be taken to The Med (medical evaluation). She doesn't want to go and says she feels fine. He says evenly that it's no longer her choice. "Once the paramedics are called, you must go and be examined."

When The Med is the destination, a CIT officer will either take the consumer in the patrol car or meet the ambulance there. Put on the stretcher for the ride, Helena is rolled into the emergency room (ER). She is now shaking. Office Schafer signs her in as a medical team takes over. Within 20 minutes he is sitting in the patrol car completing the paperwork.

By remaining calm but insistent and listening courteously, the CIT officer responded as a leader. He's able to find out what happened, send the consumer to the appropriate facility for medical assistance, and perhaps prevent a suicide. As a trained CIT officer, Officer Schafer has kept Helena out of the criminal justice system. The community provides the most appropriate and effective resources at great savings. Helena gets the attention and treatment she needs, and Officer Schafer is back on the job in the community, doing what he does best. Everyone wins.

Perceived Difficulties of Implementation

Practitioners are all too aware of and frustrated by the difficulties of implementation, so most good ideas never get proposed. Observation of CIT sites in North Carolina reveals the repetition of resolving similar issues.

Specifically, implementation struggles involve these categories:

- *Leadership* – Lacking ongoing collaborative leadership. A municipality gets in the habit of taking a service idea straight to providing it as quickly as possible. Planning a CIT program for permanence takes lengthy and detailed preparation. This involves recruiting leaders and training them to be as collaborative as possible.

- *Capacity* – Underestimating the essential functional capacity required to provide a service. This book takes great care to explain why so many local service projects don't do well. Essentially, it's a problem of not putting the supporting infrastructure for a service in place upfront.

- *Scope* – Overstating scope in an inadequate visioning process. In the heady days of clarifying vision, mission, and goals, it's common to be enthusiastic about what the team can accomplish. Experience demonstrates that starting small and progressing incrementally is the best strategy for success. Beware of over-promising and under-delivering.

- *Analysis and evaluation* – Confusing analysis with evaluation instead of combining them. Analysis determines effectiveness, whereas evaluation determines process efficiency. Combined, they reveal how and how well your program and staff are doing.

- *Resources* – Developing narrow silo resources instead of comprehensive matrices of resources. The matrix can include such resources as volunteer time and in-kind contributions targeted to the problem. It takes much more than money to make a local service project work.

- *Performance* – Mistaking workflow for measurable performance. Often analysis simply measures "low-hanging fruit." The best example is counting the number of students attending a class without finding out if they learned anything, let alone applied their knowledge to do measurable good for themselves and those served.

- *Staff* – Misunderstanding how to develop staff into a true, creative, goal-directed team.

With a sincere desire to advance justice and the common good, forward-thinking leaders come together to solve community problems. The pooling of experiences and resources now facilitates and enhances these efforts.

Taking CIT from Discussion to Reality

What is the most realistic action the criminal justice, advocacy, and mental health communities can take? How can they best divert people living with mental illness from the criminal justice system and return them to productivity in the community? The answer is to grow the idea of CIT at the grassroots level—on a neighborhood-by-neighborhood, city-by-city, county-by-county basis—one local management authority, one police department, and one sheriff's office at a time.

Currently, those interested in beginning a jail diversion program must wade through volumes of information that talk *around* the business of realizing the idea. This information needs structure to be practical.[21] *Decriminalizing Mental Illness* provides a sequential process. This includes building business support for CIT, strategic planning, evaluation, and funding justification. It suggests practitioner-based answers to the obstacles of implementation.

"Without this [process reconstruction] step, programming and services for the most marginalized of populations are left without hope and stifled in their ability to help those in need. By working in partnership with those who have the skills in critically analyzing a setting by engaging with multiple barriers and those in the community who strive to provide the best service [based on capacity], best [the most effective and practical] practices can be implemented."[22]

Getting Past Implementation to Overall Reentry Success

As mentioned, the most significant problem with starting any program is getting past the implementation phase.[23] Obstacles of implementation stop or hamstring many programs. Finding a path through these difficulties is thorny. Implementation is new with every startup—even with a proven model. The process requires a change in thinking about delivering a service.

The CIT process marks a fundamental change ***from***—

- single-agency thinking ***to*** a *matrix* of agencies organized around problem resolution;
- top-down, silo, command-and-control approaches ***to*** *bottom-up* mustering of local capacity and a street-level view of how the program is working out;
- procedure (a one-time event) ***to*** *process* (a continuous progression);
- what to do ***to*** *how* to do it; and
- mere agency compliance ***to*** involvement in *idea development* for the betterment of the community.

The literature and stories of how various programs began don't follow a prescribed sequence of how to get from one step to the next. Rather, they're a confusion of "best practices" that may be "best" for one location but not for another. Or, they're "evidence-based" practices that worked in one place, at one time, with a given set of circumstances. There's little to no attempt to put the suggested best or effective practices into context.[24] Transferability is sketchy. Chaos ensues. Thus, programs become a matter of handling the crisis of the moment. The truths for one site must be recalculated with each program. The threat remains of fading away or even dramatic failure after a number of people have invested considerable time, effort, and resources.

With a program's failure comes stigma. Trying to get another idea started after the flameout will be like trying to light the barbecue again after you've run out of propane. There has to be a way to hedge the chances of success. Thus, the work of this model is to outline the sequence of proven, practical actions that take a CIT program to decriminalize people living with mental illness from concept to self-renewing social transformation.

CIT can ameliorate—but not fully solve—the problem of large numbers of people living with mental illness caught up in the criminal justice system.[25] Therefore, sufferers are subjected to other options, which include short-term incarceration or a quick return to the street. Government assistance may be available, but it's temporary and conditional to avoid creating dependency.[26] Further complicating the problem, the system is predisposed to react to a consumer's crisis in the way things have always been done. In extremes, this leaves consumers on their own or with an ill-prepared family.

The 2002 Council of State Governments Consensus Project tracked 30 individuals to determine how resources were allocated. It found that $1.1 million in criminal justice and hospital expenses were saved by steering those individuals to appropriate community-based resources. True, expenses were transferred to other institutions and the private sector, *and* the result was far more efficient and cost-effective. Limited local public means were much better allocated. Beyond conserving resources and saving money, mental health consumers were assisted back to productivity.

One Answer, Not THE Answer

The answer to reducing the incarceration rates of mental health consumers is complex.[27] Reducing these rates is a matter of accomplishing the following:

- *Rewriting policy* – establishing a new policy to address prison/jail overcrowding
- *Improving services* – efficiently delivering mental health services
- *Reforming prisons/jails* – taking a new look at how prisons and jails are designed and function, so the incarceration experience is restorative as much as possible. This philosophy recognizes that many of those suffering from mental illness can lead functional lives in the community.
- *Enhancing pre- and post-bookings* – expanding pre- and post-booking practices to redirect the mentally ill to community public, private, and nonprofit services and care.

All of these are large areas of study. CIT is not *the* answer to reducing jail/prison populations of the mentally ill. It's one of the solutions that comprise a comprehensive local reentry strategy.[28] Why is it a *good* one? Because the idea is replicable, cost-effective, and efficient.[29] While implementing any public service program is complex, CIT lends itself to study and description because it's a definable entity; it has a purpose, a beginning, and a way to achieve self-perpetuation. Any community with a will to do so can have a CIT program.

Researching Successful CIT Programs to Create a Model

A primary task of this model is to make certain its ideas, practices, and actions apply as much as possible to various locales, sites, and stakeholders. The result is a process organized by the life cycle of project development, not *the* process of developing a

CIT project. To reiterate from Volume I: *Building Capacity from the Bottom Up: The Key to Sustaining Local Services,* the life cycle concept is easy to remember and apply to problem solving.

Everything has a life cycle, including a lawnmower—yes, a lawnmower. Buying it is only the start; it must be used, maintained, repaired, and eventually disposed of to make room for a new model. Likewise, every service idea to solve a local problem begins with an idea. You then move to planning, implementation, operation, stabilization, and self-sufficiency.

What's the difference between project implementation and process implementation? A project has a beginning and an end. A process begins with Capacity Building and aims to create an answer to a problem that evolves as necessary for as long as the problem persists. In the case of a service idea such as capacity-built CIT, you reach a goal and then create a new one in response to dynamic realities and your increased understanding of the needs. You continually update ideas along the way based on the situations you face.

So, although your process, like mowing the lawn season to season, is long-term, you continually update your "mower." You go through cycles, yes, but if you do it right, your program itself never dies because it's a process. It becomes a permanent answer to a local need for as long as that need exists, continuously building capacity to meet the changing dynamics of the problem it addresses. Some local public sector problems will never be "solved," but they can be addressed rationally.

Application of the model will require significant tailoring. Each locale must meet the needs of the unique stakeholders attempting to provide a pre-booking service for the people living with mental illness.

> "From the police perspective, developing CIT officers via CIT specialty training gives officers a new level of expertise. Empowering law enforcement officers to recognize citizens in a mental health crisis goes a long way. A true CIT officer is supported by his/her agency and local mental health services, public and private. A true CIT program creates a streamlined process for the CIT officer to assist those in need. Most important, the CIT officer is the first on the scene and must be equipped, trained, and supported to immediately make the best decision for the consumer. The last resort should be an arrest."
>
> – Christopher Hoina, Sr., Retired, Cary,
> North Carolina, Police Department

This CIT model was created as a result of a rigorous qualitative study based primarily on interviews and site visits.

Stakeholder Interviewees

The sites and interviewees selected represent the three primary stakeholder groups of CIT:

- Policing – This group represents sworn officers directly involved in either CIT training or delivering the CIT services in the course of their jobs. It also includes law enforcement executives who were instrumental in bringing CIT to their municipality.
- *Mental health professionals* – This group is comprised of professionals from Local Management Entities (LMEs),[30] the operational structure of the North Carolina Division of Mental Health, Developmental Disabilities, and Substance Abuse Services. It encompasses CIT coordinators, crisis response staff, and LME executives. Mental health professionals were interviewed via a tested questionnaire.
- *Advocates* – Advocates represent those living with mental illness, their families and peers. They were chosen based on their history of involvement with CIT. Advocate interviewees were involved with CIT from its conceptualization at the Memphis Police Department.

Other practitioners/professionals were interviewed to clarify a question or point of interest. This group included staff from jails, the North Carolina Division of Mental Health, courts, and corrections. Further, select CIT-involved practitioners from other states were contacted. They provided more information and an overview of how they tackled the difficulties of implementing the intervention. Overall, 23 people were interviewed, including the interviewees from the above stakeholders list.

Site Visits

Study sites were chosen for geographic dispersion, services offered, and willingness to participate in the study. In North Carolina, 24 LMEs cover all 100 counties. The CIT Advisory Committee recommended six LMEs that have established CIT programs and a mental health crisis capability essential to CIT.

Three LME sites were chosen as study sites. Each has a history of successful CIT services delivery, represents a cross-section of demographics, and is dispersed over large metropolitan, urban, and rural areas. Each also has crisis response capability by either a mobile team or a 24/7 drop-off facility. These sites include:

- Five County Mental Health Authority, Henderson, NC
- East Carolina Behavioral Health, Pitt County, NC. Now Trillium.
- Wake County Mental Health, Wake County, NC

Screening of the initial six sites helped to assess the following:

- *Project maturity* and progress through the three phases of the program life cycle
- *Sophistication* (e.g., staffing, services, and organizational structure)
- *Program characteristics* (e.g., measures of success, funding, and the service environment)

Focusing the Model on Jail Diversion

According to practitioners, their purpose was to clarify, even simplify, how best to make a CIT proposal work. The scope of what to study had to be precise to avoid a complicating proliferation of "good" or "urgent" suggestions not germane to what successful CIT staff have proven. Thus, this model focuses on jail diversion and decriminalizing the mental health consumer before arrest via the law enforcement-based CIT model, which is its purpose anyway. After all, the idea is to avoid the criminal justice system except in the few cases where it's appropriate.

True decriminalization of those in need of mental health services entails a range of services beyond the scope of this program.[31] Although CIT represents only one part of the required services to decriminalize the mental health consumer, it's the only pre-booking intervention and key to keeping the mental health consumer out of the criminal justice system.

Thus, research was limited to the life-cycle phases of a community-based CIT program development: Plan and Implement, Operate and Stabilize, and Sustain and Expand. It didn't include process descriptions of other interventions or agencies.

The process was narrowed to an overview of the critical features, including the following:

- *Process development* – Usually local services are seen as a terminal project, whereas focus on process targets permanence.
- *Leadership* – Leaders, usually the executive director and board, are chosen for their ability to contribute to critical functions, not necessarily their position in the community.
- *Capacity assessment* – The capacity to deliver the service in question is as important, or perhaps more important, than the service. Without an understanding of what it takes to deliver the service, urgency and excitement leads to overreach and eventual diminishment of potential.
- *Scope* – This involves thorough consideration of how *little* needs to be done so that resources aren't stretched, if not broken. It's the antithesis of the usual unrealistic wish. Preserving the *realization* of the idea is paramount.
- *Analysis/evaluation* – Again, analysis is about effectiveness—what's actually being achieved. Evaluation is about efficiency—how well it's being done. Both allow leadership to adjust processes and goals. Most of all, the picture they paint needs to justify the existence of the program.
- *Resources development* – Normally, this means securing money, but it's much more than that. It encompasses, minimally, in-kind contributions, especially labor, and donations of office space, furniture, and IT. Further, it means developing reliable funding streams from public, private, and private nonprofit sources. It may include justifying permanent local (tax-based) funding. Depending largely on grants doesn't work.
- *Services* – Usually other services are necessary to support the core service.
- *Human resources development* – The traditional approach to human resources development focuses on the individual and accomplishing tasks. The philosophy and methods of true Capacity Building centers on developing staff to collaborate, with the philosophy that the whole is greater than the sum of its parts. This approach is process focused and goal oriented, going beyond the usual functions of human resources development.

Each of the above topics are pervasive in the literature and ubiquitous in consulting. However, when accomplished through collaboration and cooperation, each critical area of service Capacity Building takes on more productive characteristics, purposes, and dimensions.

The overall goal is community betterment so families can live, work, play, and pursue happiness in an atmosphere of well-being.

This book, then, is about the metamorphosis of these features through each phase of the program life cycle. The overall goal is community betterment so families can live, work, play, and pursue happiness in an atmosphere of well-being. In other words, people can thrive.

The overall goal is community betterment so families can live, work, play, and pursue happiness in an atmosphere of well-being.

The resulting model describes the complete process of developing a local CIT program as thoroughly and practically—and as briefly—as possible. Local CIT champions can take it from there.

In Summary So Far

Each idea presented in this practical model created from research is proven by people delivering a CIT program. However, every program is unique, and there's no such thing as a "best practice."[32] What works, even in the adjoining neighborhood, is not guaranteed to work in yours. That said, these ideas are:

- *Right* - They can help others avoid the mistakes of those already developing or running CIT programs.
- *Productive* - They have elements of efficiency and effectiveness.
- *Performance oriented* - They help accomplish long-term dynamic goals.
- *Practical* - They're doable.
- *Transformative* - They lead communities to ameliorate the problems of unnecessarily criminalizing people living with mental illness.

You can have confidence in the ideas expressed in this model: They've been proven at the street level, or worm's eye view, at multiple sites over the years that CIT has been a reality. However, take each idea with the intent of modifying it both *before* using it and especially *after* the idea is working. The model can be used to strengthen an existing program as well as develop a new one. Reality is the best teacher. Ideas will need to evolve, even after a CIT program has been operating and enjoying successes for years.

No Obstacles, Only Objectives

Why have these ideas been successful? Those who suggested them adhere to a philosophy observed in all the interviews: They continually *looked beyond the problems they encountered to the objectives they sought to achieve.*

Frequently remind your stakeholders that the primary task is building service delivery capacity. The building blocks of a good idea are as important, and perhaps more important, than the idea itself. No idea can exist without a good foundation—and the strongest foundation in developing and implementing Crisis Intervention Teams rests on the political and collective will to make a difference.

... The strongest foundation in developing and implementing Crisis Intervention Teams rests on the political and collective will to make a difference.

Do You Accept?

Your invitation is not only to use this CIT model to help save lives and improve your community and its governance. It is also to develop *yourself* and your team to see the vision in decriminalizing mental illness.

The will to win, the desire to succeed, the urge to reach your full potential . . . these are the keys that will unlock the door to personal excellence.
- Confucius

Chapter 2

THE CIT CAPACITY BUILDING MODEL – MORE THAN A GOOD IDEA

Chapter 2

THE CIT CAPACITY BUILDING MODEL – MORE THAN A GOOD IDEA

Mobile Crisis Response

Finally, the consumer can say, 'I am more than my illness' and be guided to realize this truth."
– CIT Officer

Generally, local service programs that succeed have certain commonalities. First a nucleus, a local network of driven people, seizes upon an idea to make a difference. Initial champions develop a philosophy of no obstacles, only answers, or as stated by a Local (mental health) Management Entity (LME) CIT director, "Success is the only option."

The initiators intuitively see that all progress is based on relationships, so even before the idea takes hold, they set about building connections. They begin with the desired result in mind as they see that operational Capacity Building is how their idea can become socially transformative. Then they methodically put that capacity in place.

Making CIT Work

Participants in a CIT program know they are part of the reform movement to deliver public services from the bottom up. In this process, a network in the local community defines the problem and determines and implements the solution. Initiators are enthused, collegial, inquisitive, driven, serious, analytical, and above all, persistent. All are willing to work years to begin to see fruition of the program. They are committed leaders.

- *Timeliness* – Follow planning with action so there is forward movement vs. stagnation. The latter can lead to participants questioning or doubting the validity of their efforts—a sense of futility. Maintaining momentum equates to progress or the perception of it. Timeliness is a major theme of this book. It takes an action-oriented checklist and timeline for implementation, which compels timely action.

- *Salesmanship* – CIT success is a matter of salesmanship—ensuring participants in the process and others recognize the features, values, advantages, and benefits. Motivators keep their program visible to the stakeholders and the community at large by building momentum for the program kickoff. First, they understand the needs of those they serve in their CIT program, then the needs of others in their wider circle of stakeholders. Then they work to fill those needs. They see everyone who touches the idea or is the beneficiary of its services as a salesperson. A client at an intake has been known to get a program brochure for friends.

In this process, a network in the local community defines the problem and determines and implements the solution.

- *"The buck stops here" attitude* – According to one LME CIT coordinator, success begins with partners who are receptive to the idea that "the buck stops here." They're resolute in their desire to make things happen and work earnestly to correctly identify barriers and what needs to be done to get beyond them. Partnerships are cemented proactively. Expectations are set from day one. Somehow, building an idea for permanence demonstrably reduces ego.

- *Collaboration* – Leadership is a communal, collaborative effort. A sense of "we" results in less jostling for position and preeminence in a conversation and more sharing of tasks. Few duties are assigned. People are eager to help the core implementation group and willingly share the workload. A prominent sheriff once rose from a sick bed to attend a board meeting.

- *Reciprocity* – Reciprocal give and take of teaching and learning and helping and being helped are evident. People enjoy the personal growth that comes with supporting a vital, vigorous, valued idea.
- *Sustainability* – Key people think ahead and ask hard questions about sustainability and becoming operationally self-renewing. They know how they want to make a difference in a specific community and seek to understand the limits of that community's resources and dynamics. They want to get the most from what's available. And they do!

What CIT Can and Cannot Do

CIT champions understand what CIT can and, especially, what it cannot do for each stakeholder group.

- *Advocates* – Mental health advocates come to understand how law enforcement is the first line of defense for a mentally ill person. They learn that police and sheriff's deputies are indeed compassionate and concerned about all citizens. Advocates also learn the limits of what the criminal justice system, especially law enforcement, can and cannot do. They see it's better to obtain mental health services in the community than put a consumer in jail unnecessarily. They understand that their goal of helping consumers begins with the correct decision in the street, in the moment of need.
- *Mental health professionals* – Mental health professionals understand that CIT is vital to facilitating consumer access to their services and getting them initially involved in helping clients, even if it's as simple as connecting a client to a family member.
- *Law enforcement professionals* – The law enforcement community, when exposed to CIT, learns that the program is not social work. However, it can save tremendous amounts of time, money, and resources, while keeping the people living with mental illness out of jail. These professionals come to see CIT as an effective tool to (re)allocate scarce resources. Officers spend less

time on calls and maintaining the chain of custody for a mentally ill citizen. They can access resources in the community for the consumer in the course of a call for service. Collectively, officers come to realize that "CIT is not "soft on crime," but rather "smart on crime," as a crisis center director puts it. Smart community-based, performance-oriented, and data-driven policing is, in fact, tough on crime. And that's CIT.[33]

In addition, officers gain a greater awareness of the habits and ten-dencies of various mental health consumers. For example, a law enforcement officer who has been on a beat for a while knows that delivering a particular consumer to family is best.

Most important, officers gain respect. The community appreciates intelligent, compassionate policing that's tough on crime.

- *All stakeholders* – Stakeholders understand the essential value of CIT as a tool of the law enforcement entity. CIT trained officers can de-escalate a situation, which then opens many possibilities beyond arrest. Once trained, officers understand the mentally ill on a deeper, more compassionate level and realize the criminal justice system is not the only alternative for them.

Original program champions advocate CIT because it can make progress with exceptionally difficult and plaguing problems. They noted that many consumers were in jail for minor offenses and, once in jail, they didn't fare well. CIT is the right thing to do. It unifies the community and disparate agencies and services; it keeps the community safer, and neighbors feel a greater sense of security.

Dynamic and Adaptable

As it's currently developed, CIT is adaptable not only to a crisis situation for a mental health consumer but also for other calls for service, especially where de-escalation is needed.

Each of four CIT study sites adapted to jurisdictional needs by focusing on a particular emerging problem, such as teen self-destructive behaviors. The sites adapted to rural needs with a multi-jurisdictional approach.[34]

When the CIT idea first takes hold, stakeholders recognize the dynamism of the program. It continually evolves. Thus, people working on the program are always adapting to and learning from the ebb and flow of all factors involved. These include client populations, partners, services, decision makers, obstructionists, champions, and resources (money and especially donations, in-kind contributions, and voluntary work). Stakeholders understand their roles as change agents and "friends" of the program.

One CIT coordinator said stakeholders initially "inhaled" information. A shared vision came into being. Law enforcement, mental health professionals, and advocates now see the potential for collaboration where little existed before CIT was implemented.

When the CIT idea first takes hold, stakeholders recognize the dynamism of the program. It continually evolves.

Finally, the consumer can say, "I am more than my illness," be guided to realize this truth, and become a valued part of their community according to their potential.

Smart Things to Do to Prepare for CIT

Again, there's no guarantee that what works in one locale will work in yours. Any idea must be proven where it's to take root. However, much can and must be learned from past experiences. The action items, especially the Effective Practices suggested here, have been tested in a variety of settings over time. They work. Still, you will have to modify them to meet your local realities.

Life Cycle of Program Development

With that in mind, planning needs to be methodical and follow the life cycle of program development. Repeatedly, CIT experts express some form of the wisdom that "reality happens." Begin with the end in mind, i.e., decriminalizing the mental health consumer, which contributes to community well-being. Then, given your community's capacity to accomplish this objective, focus on the entire process of getting there. The survivability of an idea relies on applying the old wisdom of "less is more."

A vital part of limiting the scope of your project is knowing what you are trying to solve. It helps to fully understand the problem, which is facilitated by thoroughly answering three questions:[35]

- *Motivation* – What forces are driving current efforts to improve the law enforcement response to people living with mental illnesses?
- *Data* – What data can planning committee members examine to understand the factors influencing law enforcement responses to people living with mental illnesses?

- *Limitations* – What are the data limitations of determining the effects of mental illness on crime and improvements in community well-being, for example, and how can they be overcome?

While you're in the stage of conceptualizing how CIT will look for your municipality, practitioners suggest a certain mindset and practical things to do. Becoming aware of what CIT is while you develop a feel for the realities of your service area helps you prepare for the crucial planning process. Public program planning is largely misunderstood and improperly undertaken, if not ignored at the program's peril. Don't make that mistake.

First ensure the community has the will and resources to establish a CIT program.

- *Understand the basic premise of CIT.* Realize that CIT is a bottom-up idea. It evolves from the community, not agencies with a top-down business model. First ensure the community has the will and resources to establish a CIT program.

- *Organize the partners.* The immediate stakeholders must come from law enforcement, mental health professionals, and mental health advocates, in that order. As law enforcement officers are the first on the scene of a call for a consumer, they must be supported by their department hierarchy and be specifically recruited, fully trained, and motivated to use CIT. Beyond that, successful CIT staff suggest inviting critical collaborators with expertise as well as partners who can provide resources. (Read on for examples.)

  Always look for a spark of passion and the willingness to take communal direction in potential program participants. Beware the "visionary" who conjures up more for the many to do, whether or not it's doable. You have the vision, the problem-solving idea—in this case, CIT. That's plenty! You want inspired, even tireless, workers who can think, seek collaboration, take direction, and lead when appropriate. You want proven team members who are inspired by this work.

- *Collaborate with teams the right way.* This first group of champions should be "door openers." Aside from using practical talent from their career expertise, whether they're service providers or advocates, they need to connect to decision makers in the community. These decision makers—especially those in charge of the purse strings—will decide the fate of the program.

Although CIT does much, much more, time and money saved, in that order, are the initial motivating returns.

- *Develop a message.* Foremost, the CIT message needs to appeal to law enforcement. CIT saves time for law enforcement officers by getting them back on the beat as quickly as possible. It saves money by diverting consumers from jail. Although CIT does much, much more, time and money saved, in that order, are the initial motivating returns.

- *Design your program from alternatives.* Study the literature. You can refer to the Appendix of this book for a start. Each program will be an amalgam of alternatives to build your unique service delivery capacity and muster your unique combination of local services. Studying the literature will enable the team to know what it's trying to accomplish. More important, it will help the team know what combination of ideas and action items are most relevant for their particular area.

- *Visit sites.* Site visits provide alternate ideas all through the program life cycle and are most informative. A visit to a functioning CIT site is always better than a phone call or an email alone. It's vitally important to begin meeting CIT practitioners and gathering ideas and products already being used; so if possible, visit working, productive sites. Likewise, if you can attend an annual conference sponsored by CIT International, it's worth considering. The enlightened founder of an adult reentry program, for example, made it a point to visit other sites implementing his model—not to teach them, but to learn from them so he could continue to improve. Now that is leadership.

- *Plan for crisis response.* CIT is based on a "no-refusal" alternative to jail. The ultimate CIT service would include a 24/7 drop-off center, either stand-alone or at a hospital. Mobile crisis response teams are a good alternative to a drop-off center, but it's most effective to combine the two approaches.

It's vitally important to begin meeting CIT practitioners and gathering ideas and products already being used; so, if possible, visit working, productive sites.

- *Plan to collect data.* Make collection, analysis, and dissemination of data a foundation of your program. This develops the "picture" of productivity to continuously justify your work. Data is as crucial as it is difficult to assemble. Don't take on too many measures at first and add one only when it helps determine efficiency and/or effectiveness. Start with a few basic measures of time and cost savings facilitated by jail diversions. Make data collection, analysis, recommendations, and reporting as simple as possible and build them into daily operations upon implementation. When implemented immediately and with intent, they become routine and motivating when you see results.

Make data collection, analysis, recommendations, and reporting as simple as possible and build them into daily operations upon implementation.

- *Plan for permanence.* Developing the capacity to be self-renewing must be a major goal from inception. Planning for operational resources, for example, is long-term work that begins as an essential initial activity. Stabilizing a program is a necessary interim goal as you expand to meet true community needs, and planning for permanence is a matter of incremental growth. Take one bite at a time, and don't bite off more than you can chew and assimilate.

- *Set goals.* Again, goal setting is fundamental to an effective program. Your initial goal will be to schedule the first CIT class. Most established CIT programs began with a goal of training at least 20 percent of sworn officers in their catchment area. This goal is a challenge, especially in rural areas where law enforcement departments are small; yet it's realistic.

- *Have kickoff events.* Keeping stakeholders and citizens informed and involved builds relationships that will, in time, support and grow your CIT program. Events also reinforce the credibility of the process when others witness who else is engaged. Get the media involved. Invite any and all stakeholders, including potential partners and collaborators.

- *Recognize successes.* As part of their marketing plan, staff at successful programs have implemented recognition of almost anything that indicates the program is going in the right direction. These celebrations of success counteract negativity and stereotypes regarding the mentally ill. Not only do they submit the program for awards, but as a sign of smart marketing, they have a local decision maker, such as the chair of the county commissioners, accept the award. The award banquets recognize the stakeholders and also (and especially) the "worker bees."

Keeping stakeholders and citizens informed and involved builds relationships that will, in time, support and grow your CIT program.

- *Take action.* Nothing happens without deliberate action. Plan, yes. Then there comes a collective realization that it's time to do the thing. Don't wait for all the data and the perfect time; they never come. Reality will signal the next step.

Preparation for implementing the program plants seeds. The care director and CIT champions invite peer-to-peer discussions. They're ready for action when law enforcement is engaged, and they don't give up when faced with bureaucracy, inertia, and obstructionism. These initial preparations are only an introduction to building a program that functions well.

Now let's jump into planning for each of the critical phases of your program.

"There's as much risk in doing nothing as in doing something."
– Trammel Crow

Chapter 3

PHASE I. PLAN AND IMPLEMENT

Chapter 3

PHASE I. PLAN AND IMPLEMENT

Hill Country's Mobile Mental Health Office, Redding, California

"It is the long history of humankind (and animal kind, too) that those who learned to collaborate and improvise most effectively have prevailed."
– Charles Darwin

Don't cut planning short. The success of a program is in direct proportion to the attention paid to thinking things through. Resist the pressure to get something going quickly. Also recognize that nothing happens until you act with reasonable detail and foresight. Not perfect, just enough.

When will you know you've done enough planning? According to successful CIT practitioners, the group will sense it knows enough, has gathered enough resources, and has achieved enough buy-in to confer confidence. They also realize that only action will determine where the plan needs to go next.

Launching the program is not clear-cut. Some aspects of planning will continue into operations, and operations will continue into the sought-after stabilization, sustainability, and expansion phases. Progressing through the life cycle of your program is never-ending work. When certain goals are reached, they provide a clearer view of what more you need to plan, do, analyze, and do again in a never-ending virtuous cycle. While you'll have a sense of readiness to begin, "Starting is always a leap of faith," according to a local NAMI advocate. It's exhilarating to jump.

Tragically, CIT is often initiated because of an unfortunate event that shakes the community. A misfortune, perhaps even a death, causes the community to ask *Why?* And *What can we do?* Enough is known and proven about CIT that a tragedy need not be the reason to establish the program. However, many times CIT is thrust center stage as *the* solution with the unrealistic expectation that it's only a matter of training sworn first responders. Unfortunately, sustaining CIT is more complicated—so much so that the more plodding process of building a CIT program may be given short shrift. Avoid the trap of unnecessary expediency. Significant obstacles exist, such as a need for a 24/7 emergency response and funding, but answers arise when diligence prevails.

Obtaining Buy-in from All Stakeholders

Organizers face the initial difficulty of obtaining buy-in from all the stakeholders. Buy-in is more important than funding because nothing happens without support. Law enforcement stakeholders need to gain confidence in the program. They're often legitimately concerned that another program will take time away from regular duties. Or, they may look at CIT as doing "social work" for consumers, which is something quite different from assigned enforcement duties and responsibilities.

Those are old stereotypes; CIT is good policing. For example, CIT keeps line officers on the beat in the community. How? When confronted with a mental health consumer crisis, officers are trained to effectively de-escalate it and expeditiously guide the consumer to community services or, as a last resort, custody.

Advocates may not fully understand police procedures. However, when advocates and service providers collaborate in planning a program and participate in training, most concerns dissolve.

Mental health staff may be concerned that starting a crisis center will be cost prohibitive and too difficult to implement. Perhaps a mobile crisis unit can be set up as an interim measure before starting a crisis center, or several municipalities can share the expenses of starting and operating one.

A big complaint is that money isn't available for the program. An answer? CIT training can be provided with existing resources. Training is usually borne by the law enforcement agency; it's expensive when considering tuition, subsistence, shift coverage, and miscellaneous costs. But costs can be shared. Or, consider certified training online. Such an alternative helps make CIT training for officers and staff more sensible and realistic. However, 16 of the 40 hours required for certification must be classroom-based for the sake of discussion, role playing, and other interactions.

Advocates may not fully understand police procedures. However, when advocates and service providers collaborate in planning a program and participate in training, most concerns dissolve.

When program champions adopt a *can-do* attitude, they see no obstacles, only answers. The collaboration inherent in forming a CIT program allows a crisis center director to adopt the goal of eliminating criminal justice involvement. This goal is achievable because mental health services are made available to the consumer in the community. As one advocate observed, "It is always better to get fractured services in the community than it is to go to jail."

You'll always find a rational, productive answer to problems when the focus is Capacity Building for community betterment.

Nurturing and Growing Key Leadership

A matrix of leaders is critical to CIT's success. The National Criminal Justice Association conducted a study to determine the major reasons public programs fail.[37] Those reasons can be traced to leadership. According to the study's authors, program leadership ". . . cannot be sustained without the support of local political leaders, including legislators, court officials and the faith-based community."[38] Many more leaders than usual are essential to CIT because it requires an extensive network of stakeholders to put together a matrix of services for mental health consumers.

Overall Leadership Characteristics Desired

Following are practical leadership characteristics common to successful program leaders as they are adapted to CIT, according to the study:[39]

- *Skill to clearly communicate the vision and stick with it* – Leaders must embody, articulate, and publicize the program's vision. It's not enough to state what the champions want to accomplish. The vision needs to be realistic but challenging as well as measurable in terms of the capacity to deliver CIT services. That is, it's not enough to say the program will decriminalize the mental health consumer. It must state, for example, that decriminalization of the people living with mental illness will occur via a crisis assessment center and that the program will keep recidivism below a certain percentage of consumers served. This implies that the program will have a data process to collect, analyze, quantify, interpret, and report performance measures of the vision.
- *Passion for the program* – Repeatedly, CIT practitioners stress that success is based on relationships, which is why it's a constant point of discussion. Careful attention must be paid to those invited to participate. They must show a passion for improving the community and a demonstrated ability to do the considerable work. The idea person is short-lived because the work of implementing CIT quickly moves to the real, time-consuming, even grinding tasks of implementation. Those involved need to make daily sacrifices to produce long-term results.
- *Ability to keep the program simple* – Participants are tempted by the real and exciting possibilities of CIT to want to do too much. It's best to keep the design, processes, and procedures simple. Then you can more easily anticipate inevitable problems and address them, while minimizing many of the rest. This is a recurring theme with the successful: Learn to incrementalize as personal will and resources dictate.

Assembling Your Core Group of CIT Champions

You need a core group of change agents who are ultimately responsible for implementing CIT. This core sees that the program becomes a permanent part of local services and is socially transformative. These initial worker-leaders assemble before the wider circle of stakeholders gather. They are the glue that holds the idea intact. They can be anyone, but usually the group is comprised of law enforcement officers, mental health workers, and advocates with specialized backgrounds, education, and experience that contribute to the work of CIT. Once the idea and purpose are fixed, the dreaming ends.

This unique group needs to be small enough so members are flexible yet large enough so they can take numerous work assignments. The number depends on the talent needed for the tasks at hand. Members need to see beyond the myriad difficulties of implementation such as politics, inertia, lack of resources, silo thinking, and stereotyping; they must remain laser-focused on establishing a fully functioning diversion program. They must be organized enough so that after implementation they can operate and expand their plan. Processes and procedures, not people, are the focus, as a goal is to eventually "work yourself out of a job." No one need be so essential that their departure hamstrings the effort. This ensures a succession plan and a smooth transition to the next generation of staff.

Early on, the fewer the partners the better. A NAMI member who is part of the initial cadre of CIT champions in North Carolina recommends you add someone only as the person becomes of service to the task of Capacity Building. Add each staffer by tracing the chain of events experienced by a consumer who goes through the mental health and criminal justice processes. Each event suggests the need for a different service and talent.

Effective Practice

assemble a core group of change agents responsible for making CIT happen.

The size of this initial core group isn't crucial to success, but members must be enthused, ready to learn, prepared to commit the time, and adaptable. Thus, the culture matters, as does political support.[40]

CIT demands multitasking but avoid becoming consumed and confused by the avalanche of items clamoring for attention. Perceived "emergencies," the crises of the moment, can command the entire day's effort at the expense of doing essential Capacity Building.

Thinking in terms of the life cycle process of your CIT program helps you set daily priorities, if not strategic direction. Crises will happen; careful planning minimizes them and helps stamp them out quickly should they occur. Capacity Building helps avoid management by crisis, with which everything seems a crisis at the expense of essentials.

Begin by answering your staffing needs, especially assembling the small group of champions. This group is comprised of trailblazers who will convince their agency leadership that CIT is a cost-effective, urgent, and smart thing to do.

The best way to secure the support of key stakeholders is to have the CIT message delivered by like stakeholders. That is, a sheriff will be more receptive when hearing about CIT from a fellow sheriff or deputy.[41]

Several highly successful CIT stakeholders representing law enforcement, mental health, and CIT advocates reflected as follows on their initial fellow collaborators:[42]

- *Law enforcement* – CIT depends upon deep support from law enforcement for its existence. It takes commitment from sheriffs, police chiefs, their middle managers, supervisors, and especially line officers. A *police chief or sheriff* is the "voice of CIT." He or she embodies the leadership philosophy that "CIT begins at the top" and commits name, reputation, time, and resources for the long haul. *Middle managers* must agree the program is worthy of incorporating into operational procedures and that CIT is actually "tough on crime." Supervisors are important because they interpret the directives and assign duties. Line officers and first responders must want to be involved in the program. That is, the best CIT officers volunteer for the duty and see duty as career enhancement, which it is.

  Chiefs and sheriffs ensure that police officers and deputies attend the recommended four hours of observation at the hospital emergency department or crisis center prior to CIT certification. Each senior executive is responsible for signing and adhering to the Memorandum of Understanding (MOU—see Appendix) and designating a CIT coordinator within the agency.

  . . . The best CIT officers volunteer for the duty and see duty as career enhancement, which it is.

  The law enforcement *CIT coordinator* is responsible for attending CIT organizational meetings, maintaining a readiness checklist to accommodate all CIT training sessions, and ensuring the integrity of the CIT program.

- *Mental health providers* – This group must commit to providing crisis response that answers the needs of both law enforcement and the consumer. The local (mental health) management entity (LME in North Carolina) must ensure 24/7 drop-off capability or something equivalent for assessment and rapid assumption of consumer custody.

  Mental health professionals are most involved with CIT course content. They arrange for local instructors by topic and the four-hour clinical observation for officers. As mentioned, the latter could take place at a hospital emergency department or a crisis center. They also assist in providing classroom field-scenario role players.

Each LME is responsible for executing and complying with the Memo of Understanding (MOU) and assigning a CIT coordinator. The LME CIT coordinator reports to the senior law enforcement executive, the sheriff, or the chief, depending on the jurisdiction of the CIT program. The mental health CIT coordinator has the same general duties and responsibilities to the CIT program as the law enforcement coordinator. However, the LME CIT coordinator has the overall day-to-day responsibility for making CIT work.

- *Advocates* – Consumer advocates usually represent the National Alliance on Mental Illness (NAMI) or the local Mental Health Association. They commit to facilitating CIT within the procedural bounds of what law enforcement can provide and what mental health and the community can service as alternatives to arrest. Advocates, including consumers and their families, are involved to demonstrate the reality that a consumer is more than the illness. NAMI is usually the liaison to the community college or facility where CIT training is hosted. Liaison responsibility includes ensuring that:
    - o the *curriculum and trainers* are available for the course,
    - o *class requirements* are met,
    - o the *proper paperwork* (e.g., third-party contracts with instructors) is completed, and
    - o *end-of-class evaluations* are completed, analyzed, and used to improve the course.

NAMI representatives, with assistance from other community partners, also:

- o *set up the classroom,*
- o *schedule and assign officers for the site visits* and, to the extent possible,
- o *attend site visits* with the CIT trainees.

Site officials are community partners and conduct orientations of their responsibilities and how they fit into CIT. Advocates ensure officials are ready for students. They also set up and facilitate a consumer panel to promote spontaneous, frank discussion between consumers and officers. The purpose is to allow first responders to understand a consumer when he or she is not in crisis.

Advocates also provide refreshments during class and stage the graduation ceremony. They're responsible for signing and adhering to the MOU and designating a CIT coordinator within their organization. The advocate CIT coordinator has the same responsibilities as the law enforcement CIT coordinator: He or she is responsible for attending CIT organizational meetings, maintaining a readiness checklist to accommodate all CIT training sessions, and ensuring the integrity of the CIT program—but from the perspective of the consumer. Consumer focus helps ameliorate problems of turf tussling over program goals.

Key Qualities and Characteristics of Core Stakeholders

While it's tough to find a paragon of virtue who embodies all desired characteristics and qualities, it's ideal to have your group of core CIT champions consist of the following:

- *Risk takers* - Risk, however, is tempered with thought, care, and the realization that action must be taken, even though there's never a perfect time to act.
- *Salespeople* - Potential supporters are reluctant at first, so sales skills are a must. The work of CIT comprises constantly making, building, and cementing relationships.
- *Innovators* - This term commonly attaches to CIT champions. Here it means someone who makes things work within an existing structure and solves nearly daily problems as well as anticipates those yet to come with planning, solutions, and a little assertiveness.
- *Thinkers* - CIT champions are rational, insightful thinkers.
- *Recruiters* - Good recruiters articulate the vision in such a way that others can clearly see it as worthy of their time and efforts.
- *Leaders* - Stakeholders are reputed *leaders.* But their leadership is by example, borne of hard work and accomplishment in their respective fields.

- *Empathetic communicators* – These leaders are facile with the spoken word. They're empathetic listeners and communicators under any circumstance, from face to face to the convention hall.
- *Teachers* – Their knowledge and their communication skills make them good teachers.
- *Politicians* – These champions are effective diplomats and negotiators. They balance various expectations and also compromise and collaborate to achieve program objectives.
- *Mediators* – They are resolvers of conflict. They understand that the art of the deal is in compromise, cooperation, and collaboration, even if personal agendas taint the transaction. They find the middle ground to advance the ball.
- *Entrepreneurs* – The work isn't profitable, yet the program must show benefits to stakeholders and the community. Thus, the leaders are entrepreneurial.

You'll also want your core group to be:

- *Experienced* – in terms of decriminalizing the people living with mental illness.
- *Inspiring* – in that they can get people to do more than they thought possible, especially within this functionally and attitudinally separated group.
- *Optimistic* – meaning they see what can be achieved and how to get there rather than what's in the way.
- *Flexible* – in that they understand the few hidebound rules but are flexible in searching for and making compromises.
- *Compassionate* – not only for the target population but for the worlds of their fellow stakeholders.
- *Happy* – in terms of being generally optimistic (if not bubbly) and happy with this work.

In other words, this is a *transformative* group of leaders working on ground level for neighborhood social transformation. *Consensus builders,* they give the process of implementation time to brew. Consensus grows around the belief that there is a better way than a convenient arrest and the complications of jail.

> **. . . This is a transformative group of leaders working on ground level for neighborhood social transformation.**

Establishing Your Vision, Mission, Goals, and Values

The core group's vision, mission, goals, and values statements are vital to guiding myriad daily decisions. CIT staff commented that they referred constantly to their vision and mission when they shaped their CIT program. For example, the vision/mission helped when defining measurements and when interpreting and conducting actions in the field. Some CIT trainings incorporate nameplates for each student with CIT core values printed on the back. It's good and necessary to deeply contemplate what your CIT program is all about.

Effective Practice

State your CIT vision, mission, goals, and values as guides to daily decision making.

Vision, Mission, and Goals

A quick internet search for an article or two about the visioning process should suffice to begin developing your guiding statements. No consultants needed; you are the consultants. Following are a few examples of statements that have contributed to CIT successes. They're a good starting point—and only that. The universal wisdom from all interviewees about the visioning task is "Get on with it and get over it," meaning it's a necessary task, so give it due diligence and then move on.

Determining what your program will be and do is important beyond the obvious. Its implementation will change the community's culture from its current, institutional response to mental illness to one that incorporates community alternatives.

The examples below are borrowed from the CIT program in Moore County, North Carolina.

— Sample Vision —

CIT in [location] will enhance safety and security in the community while bringing dignity to mental health consumers.

This statement is as concise as it is noble and worthy of the work. The fact that CIT is a Crisis Intervention Team means that mental health, social services, and community alternatives are working with the courts, corrections, and law enforcement. Together, they not only help keep neighborhoods safe and secure but provide support for the people living with mental illness. The vision statement has its sights squarely on community betterment and well-being.

— Sample Mission —

The [location] crisis intervention jail diversion program promotes community well-being by reducing the involvement of mental health consumers in the criminal justice system.

This mission statement concisely specifies what CIT is (a jail diversion program), what it does (promotes community well-being), and how it does the job (by reducing the involvement of mental health consumers in the criminal justice system).

— Sample Goals —

To set a standard of excellence for the community in the resolution of conflict situations between law enforcement and people with [mental] disorders and their families.
This is done by:

- *Partnering* – Establishing collaboration among law enforcement agencies, mental health organizations, hospitals, family members, and people who suffer from [mental] disorders.
- *Educating* – Instructing officers and health professionals in how to help all consumers involved while upholding the laws of the community.
- *Promoting safety* – Ensuring the safety of everyone involved in CIT and dramatically reducing the number of people with brain disorders who are arrested and jailed.
- *Requiring responsibility and accountability* – Demonstrating individual responsibility and accountability, which are key to the success of this program.

Qualitative and Quantitative Goals

When identifying goals, you need to specify both qualitative (descriptive narrative) and quantitative (numerical) versions. Quantitative goals support the qualitative goal of furthering community well-being by measuring your progress in achieving it. These numerical goals deal with the great savings and improvements to the municipality.

The more long-term the goal, such as community well-being, the more complicated it will be to achieve, yet the more necessary it is to measure. Consider a chain of outcomes. To ensure that immediate measures lead to ultimate measures, state *immediate* measures, *intermediate* measures, then *ultimate* measures of program effectiveness in a chain of related measures.

For instance, let's say a certain number of mentally ill individuals usually end up in jail on a monthly (or yearly) basis in your community. An immediate goal might be to cut that number in half after a given amount of time employing CIT. An intermediate goal might be to reduce the number by half again (making it one-fourth of the initial number), with the goal of nearly eliminating incarceration for the mentally ill unless they've committed a crime that requires it. Enhanced community well-being is the ultimate goal of your CIT program. This can be measured by community satisfaction surveys with questions on how well people are thriving relative to decriminalizing mental health consumers.

Measure only what's meaningful to your program—and, if possible, make the measure monetizable, i.e., associate a cost with the measure. When you know the cost of an incarceration, it's easy to compute community-wide savings when a diversion is accomplished. That should help you assess the total savings realized by your program.

To ensure that immediate measures lead to ultimate measures, state *immediate* measures, *intermediate* measures, then *ultimate* measures of program effectiveness in a chain of related measures.

Let's look at how to measure partnering. Even with experiential justification, it's not enough to say that law enforcement, mental health, and advocates have successfully collaborated to conduct training. The partnership in that training must lead to something. For example, in the immediate range, it may lead to a reduction in police arrests and incarcerations of consumers. In the intermediate range, it may improve community safety and security as measured by citizen complaints. *Ultimately,* it must measurably contribute to community well-being as determined by improving mutual trust and respect between agencies and the communities served. This improvement could be measured via surveys, police reports of community response, newspaper reports or articles, and the like. Make sure your measures are relevant and goal oriented. You don't need many.

If a goal can't be quantitatively measured and have a cost component, it may not be stated sufficiently or succinctly enough to contribute to the mission.

The North Carolina NAMI senior executive cautioned that "Many wishes for the program are just that, wishes; they are simply not based in necessary data." She observed that being able to measure something is quite different from collecting the data. Goals drift back to what is immediate and easy to measure. She has seen piles of numbers collected that had no connection to the mission. For example, the number of officers who complete CIT training isn't important if that training isn't linked to reducing arrests and recidivism.

Keep in mind that the difficult part of setting a grand goal statement is that data collection and measurement are necessary to ensure progress toward that goal. This is confirmed by NAMI officials who struggle with the issue of meaningful measurement. When you're visioning, stating your grand ambition is a good start. Then work backward from the vision statement to the details of how that statement will be accomplished and measured according to the standards set by the mission. Connect community well-being with reductions in arrests then with the number of officers trained. If a goal can't be quantitatively measured and have a cost component, it may not be stated sufficiently or succinctly enough to contribute to the mission. If this is the case, either modify or discard that goal.

Make sure your measures are relevant and goal oriented. You don't need many.

Measurability is far reaching. The numbers will be used to justify the program and operational resources. Quantified results can be used to convince the skeptical that CIT is a program the community ought to fund. Again, one or two *measurable* goals showing that lives are being changed for the better are much more effective than a laundry list of unattainable goals.

Values

As the ancients observed, values indicate how the least among us are treated and mark the greatness of a society. Following are values appropriate for and relevant to CIT:

- *Compassion* – The CIT program is committed to the belief that respect and compassion are basic human needs.

- *Responsibility* - Everyone is responsible—everyone. This includes mental health consumers, who are in all but a few cases responsible for their own behavior.
- *Respect* - Every individual must be treated with dignity if a community is to be truly respectful of all its citizens.
- *Competence* - The CIT program is marked by people doing their best.
- *Community* - The community benefits by having its entire citizenry do well.
- *Social transformation* - CIT is built to be self-sustaining—to last and contribute to community well-being if the community has the will and need to decriminalize the people living with mental illness.

Combatting Inertia

Despite your grand plans and hopes for improving the community and possibly saving lives, in launching your program, you will face inertia. Each stakeholder group has functioned as a silo service for decades, and resistance to change is palpable. To that programmatic obstruction, you can add cultural stereotyping. People are used to the way things are; culture is tough to change.

Timing is important, according to NAMI officials. Determining the vision and scope of your program helps the group coalesce. It's a way to "feel when the players are ready, willing to do great things," according to a founding member of the North Carolina CIT initiative. It helps people realize that CIT is formulaic, meaning it's a relatively simple (but not easy) idea to implement—and it works, especially if it follows a proven action plan to realize the idea.

Assembling the Wider Circle

Now that you've established your core group and that group has determined your vision, mission, goals, and values, let's look at assembling the wider circle of change agents, collaborators, and partners.

Effective Practice

Assemble key stakeholders and get buy-in.

First, be aware that the list of people and agencies to consider is voluminous and can smother the leadership body with its own weight. The task, then, is one of deciding whom not to include rather than whom to include. Obviously, the mix for your community will be unique. For example, it's more difficult to assemble essential stakeholders in rural areas. Distance deters developing a tight network of productive relationships.

Form your list in ever widening circles:

- *Primary stakeholders* – First consider the primary stakeholders: members of law enforcement, mental health professionals, and advocates.
- *Resource and service providers* – The next circle includes those who provide direct resources and services. These people could be the staff at the local community college and mental health providers who will instruct CIT training. Perhaps a jail liaison would fit your program as such a person diverts the people living with mental illness from jail before sentencing. A jail liaison can also provide essential data for figuring out the cost effectiveness of the effort.
- *Overall supporters* – Then consider professionals, agencies, or groups that can help overall, such as criminal justice experts, the faith-based community, and business owners. Businesses have a vested interest in community well-being as it's "good for business."
- *The community* – The last circle is community members, who need to know about the program and how they fit into it. People in the community likely will be the ones to make a CIT call for service and can help with a possible de-escalation. It's a good idea to task team members with maintaining essential collaborative connections by exchanging relevant, timely, and meaningful information.[43]

Reminder: Everyone CIT touches is a potential advocate and salesperson for your program, especially if CIT has helped them personally. Enlist them. Have that CIT pocket card ready.

Helpful Agencies or People

The following agencies or categories of individuals were suggested by CIT practitioners as being helpful. Choose carefully, as it will take considerable work to obtain and maintain buy-in then hold the group together to get work done. A criterion for inclusion, as suggested by experienced CIT staff, is to ask, "What can this agency/person do for CIT now and, especially, further down the road?"

The people you'll want to work with will be some of the busiest people in the community. Perhaps they'll be serving on a community collaborative that will supersede work with CIT—but they need to fully commit. Also, remember that everyone asked to help can be a potential "no" vote when decisions need to be made, so an initial group of a few but determined champions is best.

Groups from which to choose can include the following:

- *Crisis response staff* – Crisis response is a separate *effective practice* of mental health services. It involves a system to take custody of the mental health consumer from the law enforcement officer and provide emergency care. Crisis response is so critical that these individuals require mention in the list of collaborators/partners. They relieve the line law enforcement officer, who is the first stakeholder in a successful CIT program. The line officer must remain on duty with as little distraction as possible as his or her first responsibility is the safety and security of the community. The line officer's sworn duties have a legal basis and are highly regulated. Having the right thing done quickly in a mental health related call for service is critical. The officer must be able to hand off the consumer quickly, safely, and to the proper care provider.

- *Mental health professionals and providers* – These include state agencies and local providers—public, private, and nonprofit. Successful CIT sites develop a reference index of services for referral. Service providers are advocates for the consumer. They provide, for example, subsistence, housing, counseling, medical treatment, residential substance abuse treatment, access to public aid, and funding. You might consider the Department of Mental Health, the Department of Social Services, the Department of Public Health, and in North Carolina, the Division of Juvenile Justice and Delinquency Prevention. These services represent a continuum of care for the matrix of assistance consumers need. Early on, service providers can help compile the quick field reference of local, accessible services and support. Places and people ready to serve unique mental health consumer needs are the heart of diversion.

Places and people ready to serve unique mental health consumer needs are the heart of diversion.

- *CIT instruction sites and instructors* – North Carolina has a reciprocal agreement with community colleges for instructional facilities and support.

Service providers are also CIT guest lecturers, so putting together a class is a way to connect to resources for the diversion effort. North Carolina is fortunate to have a network of four-year and local community colleges that provide college courses and technical training within commuting distance of nearly everyone in the state. These community colleges are convenient for CIT training because many times they already offer criminal justice courses and basic law enforcement training. The North Carolina local colleges receive fees for conducting classes, and the CIT network gets complete classroom support near law enforcement agencies. It's a win-win arrangement. Thus, contacting your local technical college is one of the first things to do to voice your intent and establish a time for the first class.

- *Area mental health services/CIT coordinator* – This person is vital. The coordinator is responsible for assisting with planning, answering the barriers to implementation, facilitating the Capacity Building process, and making CIT a permanent presence. The ideal person has considerable experience serving the mental health consumer. Perhaps he or she has run a mental health services agency, successfully navigated bureaucracies, and demonstrated proficiency as a problem solver devoted to CIT as a cause. One of the most successful CIT area coordinators in North Carolina characterized her job with "I am the how of CIT." Even after years of service, she remains enthused about the idea of decriminalizing the people living with mental illness in her catchment area of 11 counties!
- *Hospital mental health staff* – If your service area has a hospital, it may have or be able to create staff positions that augment the CIT effort with a 24/7 drop-off service. Buy-in will come when hospital staff realize that mental health care is a viable alternative to incarceration. According to an area CIT coordinator, these people are a "buck stops here" resource. Why? They are receptive to making CIT happen; they're integrated into the community; they intuitively see the benefit of CIT and how to assist its implementation; they work well with stakeholders; and they have the perspective of well-being as a goal. Consider the following:
    - *A director of behavioral health* or similarly titled person in charge of a behavioral health unit is most helpful in establishing a 24/7 drop-off arrangement.

- *A hospital liaison* is responsible for outreach. He or she helps CIT integrate into the community. The purpose of a liaison is all about building relationships, addressing systemic issues, and arranging holistic, family-centered care. This person "does what it takes." This might involve meeting people publicly or privately on their terms and turf, finding a bed, greasing the wheels of bureaucracy, or managing a consumer in need. The liaison provides a global view and the communications link needed for jail diversion by understanding and facilitating the who, what, and how of hospital operation. One hospital organized a Consumer and Family Advisory Committee with CIT in mind.
- *A triage nurse,* or quasi-case manager, accompanies the consumer from the emergency room to a bed.

- *Criminal justice professionals* – All through the process from arrest (if it happens) to jail are advocates for CIT because CIT is the only pre-booking alternative to the criminal justice system. A judge, for example, is a superior ally and "barrier remover" because he or she can divert a consumer from the bench even *after* booking. The judge can establish a mental health court as well as be a prominent cheerleader for decriminalizing the mental health consumer.
- *City and county officials* – Consider the county/city manager, who will be interested in cost savings from CIT. The savings can justify budget support for CIT. In fact, the county manager at one of the original North Carolina CIT sites helped construct, adopt, and communicate the original vision of the program. Again, it's good business.
- *Elected officials* – A strong mayor or council/commission member is indispensable as these people are well positioned CIT cheerleaders and can arrange funding.
- *Emergency response professionals* – While EMS or fire department officials may not be in on the original CIT planning, tasking, and work, they respond to consumer crises. Therefore, you eventually need to bring them into the CIT fold. It's not uncommon to have multiple agencies and providers respond to the same call, and it's helpful for all to use the same operational procedures.

- *Faith-based communities* – Churches have resources and services at their command, and it's common for them to offer a consumer respite. A church's network to potential supporters can be extensive, and its mission to help is most compatible with CIT goals. Churches suggest Christian support, but many communities have an all-faith or interfaith council.
- *Veterans' agencies* – Also, you might include veteran's hospitals/VA and homeless shelter staff, as they often identify and deal with mental health issues.
- *Businesses* – Business owners are important because they're a conduit to the community and resources. An effective CIT media sales campaign includes flyers and communiques to as many businesses as possible. One CIT executive leader frequently attends business meetings and business social gatherings.
- *The media* – The media is included not so much as a partner but as a willing participant. It's often one of the first stakeholders to be ignored, but don't underestimate this collaborator. The media can paint a brutal picture of an encounter with a consumer, or it can help tell *the rest of the story* that happens with a pre-booking jail diversion program.
- *Community groups* – Make sure to attend regular meetings of community service groups. They're a source of resources and another conduit to the community—often to the most prominent citizens.
- *Consumers and their families* – Consumers are a vital part of CIT training. It's one thing to study dealing with mental health crises from a textbook; it's quite another to hear firsthand from consumers and their families how best to respond. It helps build compassion and understanding to experience consumers when they're *not* in crisis and see them as functional neighbors.

Appeal to each group with data meaningful to their specific needs. Each one of these core partners has basic, common yet unique needs for information from the program. Often the needs stem from practical concerns about saving money.

- *A judge,* for example, is interested in how the reduction in mental health consumers seen in court saves court staff time and how much money the court saves.

- *A sheriff* is interested in dollar savings to his jail and time saved by his deputies who were previously burdened with transporting and attending to consumers.
- *A business owner* is interested in knowing the return on his or her investment (donation). For example, the owner may want to know how much crime rates will drop. Community well-being improves because such changes have a positive effect on business.
- *A hospital* is interested in savings that result from reducing the number of repeat visits to the Emergency Room and Mental Health Emergency Department.
- *Media representatives,* on the other hand, are interested in a good story, and you want to make sure it's a positive one. Invite media representatives in early and educate them on the program. Let them know someone will call whenever a newsworthy event happens. It shows respect for their services to the community.

  Include media relations as part of planning. Assign someone to handle messaging to the media, which will probably be the executive director, at least initially. The job entails:

  - making connections with and engaging media reps or reporters,
  - coordinating them and feeding them news,
  - setting up ride-alongs and media opportunities,
  - prepping spokespersons, and
  - coordinating partners so CIT has a unified voice.

All these potential supporters will appreciate a continuous, even overwhelming, flow of information about the benefits of CIT. The purpose of disseminating information is to develop friendships and acquaintances who become partners willing to meet on a regular basis.

Establishing Regular Meetings

A great deal of material on how to conduct productive meetings is available if desired. Make sure you establish "rules of engagement." Productive meetings are structured around reporting by committee members.

Effective Practice

Meet regularly in an organized fashion with an emphasis on purpose.

Make sure everyone understands the purpose of this nascent assembly:

Purpose of CIT Meetings

To be a gathering of friends united by the vision of
making CIT a permanent part of the community and
socially transformative by decriminalizing the mental health services consumer.

The work of initial meetings needs to move quickly from the animated stage of throwing around ideas to the assignment of tasks and the difficult but rewarding work of implementation. Visionaries with lofty ideas need to realize *their* ideas will require volumes of *their* time and effort over the years of work successful programs demand.

Members of the partnership should expect to meet regularly. Early on, this should be every other week to:

- *Develop common understanding and respect* – Meetings are a venue for establishing common understanding and respect, which form the foundationof a sustainable partnership. You can work out differences in understanding how to proceed before they become problems.

Meetings are a good time to discuss the ever-present VUCA (Volatility, Uncertainty, Chaos, Ambiguity) and how to deal with it without obsessing over it.

Answer: See a setback as an opportunity for improvement. If you're never stumbling, you're not learning or progressing.

- *Share information, successes, failures, and opportunities* – In meetings, you can share CIT news, which is especially important if it relates to needed changes in the training program to deal with an emerging issue.
- *Coordinate dissemination of information* – Meetings offer the opportunity to coordinate spreading information about the program throughout the community. For example, you can coordinate efforts to incorporate CIT

concepts into other professional settings, such as with EMS (Emergency Medical Services), dispatchers, and jailers.

- *Discuss and resolve problems* – Meetings also provide a discussion forum for resolving special cases and problems and taking advantage of opportunities.[44]

The champions that started the first countywide decriminalization effort in North Carolina demonstrated exceptional creativity. Besides meeting on a regular basis themselves, they made sure they were on the agenda at meetings of *other* stakeholders. They attended recurrent meetings of the police department and sheriff's office, business groups, community service clubs, and municipal groups. It's no wonder they had vigorous, vital, even viral local support for CIT *before* the first class signed up. Success resulted from their excellent planning and organization from the beginning.

Effective Practice

Organize work by functional committees and standardized operations.

What's one of the best ways to navigate myriad urgencies? Divide and conquer. Divide the workload, that is.[45] Why? This focuses the efforts of the critical functions such as building capacity, training, marketing, and developing resources and strategy. As mentioned before, daily distractions will arise that seem worthy of instant resolution—at the expense of answering the real necessities of implementation. These normal "crises" have a way of devolving into management by crisis. Guard against this by discerning what a genuine crisis is; most situations are not. For example, IT issues require attention and energy nearly daily. But are they crises? Usually not, but they can cause havoc, especially if you're preparing a key presentation at budget time.

Plan for difficulties known and unexpected, and those you didn't realize could ever happen. You know, for example, that you'll have end-of-the-month reporting crunches. A key person may quit unexpectedly. Then a liability suit might arise out of the blue.

It's the job of a morally and character driven leader to take the high road. Remaining calm supports maximum brain function and operational skill. Yes, you can expect chaos, but deal with each incident from the assurance that you and your staff can solve it. This will reduce unnecessary stress for everyone involved. Don't succumb to management by crisis at the expense of daily work on mission-critical activities.

Building capacity is one of the first necessities ignored, yet it has the most far-reaching impact. Make sure committees focus attention and man hours on long-term *key* issues. In no order of preference, consider the following committees:

- *The Capacity Building Committee* – This committee builds the foundation that supports the business of delivering services and does the following:
    - o Assesses needs to *identify* gaps in service.
    - o Determines *resources for training*, including staffing, instructors, and facility needs.
    - o Arranges *orientation visits* to clinics, hospitals, and service providers.
    - o Conducts both in-state and out-of-state *site visits* to successful CIT collaboratives, crisis assessment centers, and other diversion programs.
    - o Knows and fits CIT to the overall community *reentry strategy.*
    - o Facilitates use of the all-important *readiness* tools (Appendix: CIT Program Readiness Checklist; CIT Implementation Readiness Checklist).
- *The Policies and Procedures Committee* – A sheriff's office charter member CIT coordinator stated, "There is much to define to avoid confusion when [policies and procedures] are executed." More than likely, the first time CIT stakeholders work shoulder to shoulder for a common purpose will be to develop clear policies and procedures.

Commonality of purpose takes time and a little persuasion to nurture. Previously, stereotypes and inertia have kept these groups isolated and, in some cases, antagonistic to one another. Some of that misunderstanding still exists. Hence, it's mandatory to document how people are expected to conduct themselves in the form of operating procedures and Memorandums of Understanding. Conflict will arise simply because law, rules, regulations, and years of experience dictate the conduct of each stakeholder group. It's a matter of communicating those dictates and respecting those of others.

Consider developing the following documents upfront:

- o Procedures:
  - ■ SOPs – Standard (law enforcement) operating procedures for transferring custody of a consumer (Appendix: CIT Police Procedures: Interacting with the Mentally Ill)
  - ■ LE procedures – Law enforcement dispatch and response procedures
  - ■ *Response team procedures* – Procedures between a crisis response team/center and CIT officers
- o MOUs:
  - ■ *Stakeholder MOU* – An MOU among the three core stakeholders (Appendix: CIT Memorandum of Understanding)
  - ■ *Crisis response team MOU* – An MOU for a mobile crisis response team
- o Protocol – An emergency response protocol
- o *General order* – A general order or policy establishing CIT in a law enforcement agency (Appendix: CIT Law Enforcement Officer Policy)

These documents head off considerable misunderstanding that may end the program before the team has a chance to formalize collaborative arrangements.

- *The Training and Curriculum Committee* – This committee will have the significant responsibility of CIT training. This topic is fully addressed later.
- *Jail Diversion/CIT Oversight/Planning and Advisory Committee* – This committee may also be called the *Stakeholders Operational Committee.* It has overall responsibility for strategic planning and putting the tactics, effective practices, and action items into the unique plan and getting them working. Another vital task of the committee is ensuring that all avenues for diversion are in place. Besides CIT, a consumer can be diverted from jail through the court before sentencing. A pre-implementation plan is mandatory (Appendix: CIT Pre-implementation Work Plan).

The needs of the consumer should ultimately determine how you design and develop your CIT program.

Decriminalizing people living with mental illness is a knotty problem—and not a solitary one. For optimal results in the community and positive influence on neighborhood well-being, make it part of your reentry strategy. Make sure the CIT initiative does not stand alone. Remember: small, iterative, resolute steps.

- *The Resources Committee* – This topic will be treated in detail later. For now, know that it's critical for a committee to work on obtaining the wherewithal to implement, sustain, and expand your CIT program. Recall that developing support is mostly accomplished by establishing long-lasting friendships in the community and beyond.
- *Consumer and Family Advisory Committee* – The needs of the consumer should ultimately determine how you design and develop your CIT program. If your program only satisfies practitioners' needs, it will fail. It must better the situation of those living with mental illness, their families, and their neighborhoods.

Choose committee members by their willingness to serve on the committee in question. This means genuinely, cooperatively work toward a common goal. Keep a keen eye on the special qualifications, knowledge, and expertise required for implementation and Capacity Building, with emphasis on the latter. If you concentrate on Capacity Building, *you will* have a successful implementation phase.

Naturally, your committee structure will be dictated by the local need. One of North Carolina's early champions of CIT observed that some CIT programs may be too small to afford the luxury of several committees. Again, there is always an answer. Ask those serving to perhaps cross train and work in multiple roles. Vision- and goal-directed people often insist on handling multiple responsibilities as long as they see progress. Still, the critical functions assigned to committees should not be ignored. As you organize, keep asking, "Is this (action, policy, procedure, decision) creating capacity that decriminalizes the mentally ill?'

Developing a Strategic Plan

The best strategic plans are action oriented, flexible, organic, and decidedly long-term. The people of the organization who are developing workable, practical strategies will base them on their own thoughts, needs, and capacity. The best strategic statements are put in terms of daily activities they can measure for efficiency and effectiveness against overall goals.

Effective Practice

Develop an action-oriented strategic plan.

When strategy is action-oriented, the first strategy meeting results in action items to resolve defined problems. Specific people or entities are assigned to certain actions for completion by a particular date.

Then you'll need daily work and regular meetings, especially quarterly "pulse checks." These checks ensure you're resolving problems with a steady march to daily, monthly, yearly, and ultimate goals. Everyone is vitally involved, especially leadership, who must own the vision, mission, and goals by investing much of their daily time on each. This is where the commitment, passion, and work ethic of the leader comes in. Devising and especially enacting good strategies can't be delegated.

Organic and Flexible

Action-oriented visioning is organic in that action items are largely bottom-up ideas supported by leadership and managers. These leaders work in a loop of ground-level discussion, action, and analysis, then back to ground-level discussion. Each loop brings a higher plane of insight granted by progress.

Strategy is flexible in that it changes as dictated by reality and ground truths. You need to establish strategic milestones for the near, intermediate, and outlying years. Those milestones, when worked backward to the present, define what should be done on a daily, if not minute-to-minute basis. Working on the chain of outcomes keeps the team focused beyond the "crisis" of the moment, which maintains forward movement.

Few things are as productive as a good strategic process, yet it's regularly mishandled. Let your strategy guide you, not the other way around. The idea is to connect daily action to overall strategic goals. Without this connection it's *easy* to be quite *busy* with the *wrong* work.

Let your strategy guide you, not the other way around. The idea is to connect daily action to overall strategic goals.

Reaching agreement about basics early on is essential.[46] Goals should be broad enough for consensus and narrow enough to facilitate accomplishment. Less is more yet again. For example, a goal to reduce consumer incarceration numbers is better than one to ease the difficulties of mental health consumers; the first is measurable; the other is difficult to grasp. Maintain control by not having to chase too many seemingly worthy but unattainable results.

Let your strategy guide you, not the other way around. The idea is to connect daily action to overall strategic goals.

The guide for adopting a strategic goal and its measures is whether you can translate it into an argument to justify CIT programming and resources. Again, the best argument is how much money and time can be saved with an activity. Don't succumb to the tyranny of numbers for the sake of numbers, however. Focus on a measure or two that should satisfy each major stakeholder group. More on measurement follows under Design Impact Analysis and under Analyzing and Measuring Progress, so for now, the discussion on strategy continues.

Overview of the CIT Strategy Process

Following is a brief overview of the CIT strategy process. Each topic is treated in more detail throughout the process of implementation:[47]

- *Create a shared vision to guide daily activities.* This is a concise statement of what you want your CIT program to be to the community, not to the participating agencies. Creating your vision, mission, goals, and values has been addressed in detail earlier in this chapter.

- *Define target groups.* Obviously, the main target group is comprised of those living with mental illness, or mental health consumers. Remember, however, that equally important target groups are defined by the original key stakeholders—beyond consumers, law enforcement, and the mental health community. Consider businesses, for example. Think of your overarching goal of community well-being, of creating safe, secure communities where people can thrive.

Targeting means developing profiles of those you will serve or need as collaborators. For example, do you want to serve only consumers who have committed serious offenses? Keep in mind that focusing on minor offenses is a great opportunity to avoid more serious offenses, an arrest, and possibly an incarceration. These profiles are vital as they will determine how and what resources you deploy and how indispensable, program-sustaining relationships become refined.

- *Examine available models.* Do take time to visit other working CIT programs. Your program will be an adaptation of several sites that exemplify services, training, and response protocols.[48] Successful CIT program officials trace their success back to visits to appropriate, successful CIT sister sites (Appendix: CIT Program Resources and Key Contacts). If travel is restricted, don't hesitate to call—often. People doing CIT are most willing to help. The CIT community is a close fraternal entity that evolves.

Effective Practice

Develop project scope by mapping clientele and community resources.

- *Identify/map community-based resources.* Identifying gaps in mental health services is important. It helps you to prioritize the services that need to be filled to complete your portfolio of mental health care. That said, having a complete array of mental health services is legendarily difficult to accomplish. More realistically, understand resources by completing a services-to-needs analysis to catalog criminal justice and community alternatives to arrest. Organize all community-based services, whether or not they're specifically mental health services, in a single, quick-reference brochure.[49] This can serve as a resource for law enforcement and first responders.

- *Determine where to invest scarce resources.* Initially, focus on law enforcement training and putting a crisis response in place. Remarkable progress in offering services can be made simply from existing people, agencies, and services. Don't bite off more than your collective will and local resources can support. Once an initial cadre of first responders and infrastructure people (e.g., 911 telecommunicators) has been trained, you'll have a clearer picture of where to put limited assets for further training or perhaps personnel. For example, a successful grant proposal can result in funding a dedicated CIT officer for the sheriff's office, which is a significant piece of the diversion puzzle. Treat a grant for what it is, mana from heaven. That said, it's terminal money with strings attached. If, for example, you fund a position with a grant, make sure you have permanent support lined up before accepting the award. Hear the voice of experience.

A Helpful Handbook for Strategic Planning

To be successful, strategic planning requires commitment on the part of three entities: organizational leadership, the CIT implementation team, and a strategic planning facilitator. You can conduct strategic planning in-house (within the core group) to save funds. It would be most helpful if the job of facilitator were assigned to the most capable and *willing* person. A no-nonsense point of departure is found in *A Handbookfor Strategic Planning*.[50] This handbook presents a good take on the roles and responsibilities of each key entity and suggests a process by which these key people can point CIT toward its future.

Strategic planning is a continuous process that must be tailored to accommodate the climate of an organization and the dynamic nature of delivering public services—especially decriminalizing the mental health consumer.[51] The original planning group needs to intuit when thinking and planning must stop and action must begin. Avoid the tendency to want to know just a few more facts to be a little surer of when to act. Wisdom has it that 80 percent surety is enough, and some go with 60, even 40, percent surety when ground reality says go.

Assessing Readiness

On one hand, it seems simpler to begin CIT than most service programs: Just pick a date to begin a CIT class and have that date drive all activity. But don't be deceived by that seeming simplicity. Much of the task of CIT is changing the culture of service silos and stereotypes.

Effective Practice

Assess readiness to implement CIT.

The best way to change the culture is to establish CIT. First your group needs to understand how ready it is to take on the work. The value of a readiness checklist (Appendix: CIT Program Readiness Checklist) is that it helps focus attention on:

- relationship building,
- the mechanics of cultural change,

- the details of who is to do what and especially how,
- the difference between planning and implementation, and
- a date when enough (even if not perfect) infrastructure is in place to begin.

Your readiness instrument should be unique to your environment and keep Capacity Building, process efficiency, and program effectiveness in mind.

One of the founders of CIT in North Carolina commented regarding how the initial programs began, that "CIT [the idea] can't be improved; it has to grow from the community out."

Next in this process of Capacity Building is to understand the service delivery capacity of the locale that will host your CIT effort. So let's dig in.

Assessing Capacity

Why the emphasis on Capacity Building? It is the key to getting beyond the difficulties of implementation, which are the greatest obstacles to making good ideas work in our neighborhoods. With successful implementation, it becomes possible to make problem-solving infrastructure self-renewing. Arriving at self-renewal is a nearly magical turning point; your idea sustains itself as an answer to a vexing local social ill.

This state of program development is considerably beyond stabilizing operations. This is when a program becomes permanent, with its own resources, its own social capital, its own services, and its own funding. When an idea becomes part of or the sole solution to a social ill, it can have a lasting and positive effect on lives, thus enhancing community well-being.

Do stakeholders believe in CIT enough to bring their scarce resources to the table? Each stakeholder must see his or her specific role and how it contributes to the overall vision and mission. All stakeholders need to be respectful of, if not personally subservient to, the purposes of CIT; no one person or group on the team is preeminent. It's very much a bottom-up endeavor.

Both advocates and mental health professionals at successful sites honor the mission and legal requirements of law enforcement. Consequently, they modify their support and the construct of CIT as necessary to assist the officer on the beat when he or she responds to the 911 call for a mental health consumer.

Why the emphasis on Capacity Building? It is the key to getting beyond the difficulties of implementation, which are the greatest obstacles to making good ideas work in our neighborhoods.

According to a crisis center executive director, LME representatives need to internalize that *it's their job* to help facilitate law enforcement's role in responding to a call for service. This means providing some sort of crisis response when needed. Without crisis response where and when it's needed, the officer may have to resort to arrest. If the mental health community wants CIT, it needs to find the resources, mainly money, to solve the 24/7 crisis response dilemma.

Resources and agreements are required to transfer the consumer from law enforcement custody to mental health professionals as quickly as possible. The benefits of doing so are compelling but may not convince local officials to fund crisis response. It's expensive and means diverting money from other "necessary" general and mental health services. Still, redirecting resources can be done profitably and with significant positive impact on the consumer.

The North Carolina Five County Mental Health Authority leadership, for example, reorganized funds and set aside $750,000 to establish a crisis center. Leadership saw CIT from the perspective of law enforcement needs; they prioritized a stand-alone crisis center. Aside from saving the county money by avoiding use of the criminal justice system, the center is now fiscally sound because it correctly apportions and allocates limited local resources.

Three Capacity-Building Areas

Three overarching areas of services related to Capacity Building for a CIT program include training, crisis response, and an appropriate array of services for persons with mental illness. The first two are considered together. The proper handling of a mental health crisis is dependent on a quick transfer of custody from the CIT-trained first responder to the proper mental health professional or agency. The section in this chapter on Developing Performance-Oriented Services for Consumers fully addresses training.

The area of general community services is considered separately. Those services are developed by different means. Slow to be realized, they are always in need of bolstering. CIT works acceptably with existing alternatives to incarceration.

Preparation for Training

Preparing for the first CIT class involves determining four resources. North Carolina serves as an example. Other states and possible sites will need to consider their unique capabilities and resources.

- *Facilities* – The North Carolina network of technical colleges was planned so that every state resident would be within commuting distance of a school offering a two-year degree. These colleges provide designated classrooms and support for CIT within reasonable reach of all who need or are interested in training. Local officers attend local schools, allowing CIT to be genuinely community-based and community-wide. Capacity-building involves arranging for the colleges to provide space for the training. Experience proves they offer value to a good educational/community cause.
- *Classroom trainers* – Probably the most difficult part of conducting training is to have a full slate of mental health guest lecturers, such as psychologists, counselors, and therapists. These professionals are often volunteering and may have rather frenetic careers. Consequently, other demands frequently take precedence, and last-minute cancellations in the lecture schedule are not uncommon. In North Carolina, the LME CIT coordinator is best suited to identify mental health professionals for this task. It's wise to secure backups.
- *Staff* – Your staff will include support personnel from the facilities or community colleges and law enforcement, particularly the law enforcement school director and training coordinator. In North Carolina, technical schools conveniently provide audiovisual, janitorial, reception, and administrative help plus certifications and CEU documentation. The school is remunerated by the state of North Carolina for each student trained. Other states may have a similar arrangement for support.

  Overall responsibility for a class, which includes creating the classroom experience, belongs to CIT leaders from participating law enforcement agencies. They are supported by the LME CIT coordinator. Anything else, such as setting up refreshments, building study binders, and sponsoring the graduation ceremony, is usually handled by the advocates as initial members of the training committee.
- *Crisis response professionals* – Successful CIT program staffers established crisis response capability nearly from the first days of planning. Crisis response capability from mental health professionals must be ready well before the first CIT certified officer resumes the beat and even before the first class. Establishing a crisis center isn't necessary right away, but it's a highly advisable goal.

Effective Practice

Assess readiness to implement CIT.

Chain of Events in a CIT Call

What occurs when a mental health consumer is in need? First, the 911 dispatcher receives a call. To dispatch the correct officer, the person who takes the call must be trained to identify critical information.[52] Then, if a CIT officer is dispatched, the officer must be skilled in de-escalating the situation, understanding the person's needs, and determining the appropriate action. This action may be calling for crisis response, making a referral to services, or transporting the consumer and correctly transferring custody to, say, a hospital with mental health services. If none of these options is viable, arrest may be necessary. The consumer may not refuse whatever the officer decides.

The call for mental health service bridges the criminal justice system and the community by providing the following:[53]

- *Collaboration* – The call for service activates the matrix of law enforcement, community mental health services, and advocates.
- *Assessment* – The expeditious involvement of mental health professionals via crisis response allows an accurate assessment and correct referral to services for the consumer.
- *Care* – It initiates appropriate consumer care, which may be:
    - o *treatment,* including case management, restarting medications, and designing wraparound services, and/or
    - o *rehabilitation,* including for example, arrangements for short- or long-term housing.

"Nothing happens unless law enforcement wants it," according to a NAMI official. Translation: Law enforcement must see the benefit of bypassing the criminal justice infrastructure.

Begin early to create a viable alternative to arrest—*before* the first CIT class. The holy grail of crisis response is the 24/7 crisis assessment center. Its significant initial, and especially extended, operational costs are deterrents; however, the idea is worth pursuing. Meanwhile, a combination approach of mobile crisis response and cooperative arrangements with hospitals and clinics can allow time to explore the 24/7 alternative.

Considerations in Crisis Center Planning

An experienced crisis center director cautioned that crisis center planning needs to consider the following:

- *Public opinion* – Many people think that CIT clientele are "dangerous" and, therefore, don't want a crisis center in their neighborhood or near a school. On the contrary, such a center can prevent escalated situations. When people understand that a crisis center is good, cost-effective governance, objections diminish. Again, reason for your continuous public relations efforts.
- *Location* – Transportation can be a deterrent to access. Locate the crisis center as centrally and as near the greatest need for mental health services as possible.
- *Visibility* – People must be able to find the facility easily. Don't hide it as a nondescript office in a small strip store.
- *Zoning* – The center must be big enough to accommodate estimated consumer numbers and needs to be close to community services such as a hospital with a mental health emergency service, and/or social and mental health services. Disseminated information should stress that the center is not a clinic or a therapy center but a mental health crisis assessment center for "your" neighborhood.
- *Facility* – Will it be a new building or a renovated one? Either way, make it as welcoming, adequate, and functional as possible.
- *Role(s)* – Know what role(s) the center will play in the continuum of mental health/substance abuse services. For example, will it serve as a detox center? Will it handle people with developmental disabilities? Adolescents? Any mental health consumer involved in a law enforcement crisis? What psychiatric services will it offer? Each role has unique requirements and approaches. You will need to be specific about the role(s) of the center and that you want to represent the municipality while providing needed services.

- *Licensure* – Be prepared for a lengthy process. Contact your licensing agency early on to find out and respond to the specifics required.
- *Budget* – Personnel will be the single largest budget category. Think of the cost of a physician at $300,000+ per year and the staff it takes to support the position. The danger is in underestimating and having to request unanticipated infusions of money. The budget must be precise enough to cover expenses and forward thinking enough to anticipate contingencies without being seen as "padding" the budget request. Justifiable accuracy matters.

The holy grail of crisis response is the 24/7 crisis assessment center.

Put yourself in the seat of a budgeteer. Budgeting may not be a matter of live or die for your program, as you may have reasonably stable funding streams. However, it's about what can or can't be done. Budget prep is one of your most vital responsibilities and duties. Success should come quickly, and with that will come additional responsibilities and requirements to implement the needed services. It seems the reward for success born of good hard work on an idea whose time has come is more hard work—if you're lucky.

- *Staff* – Choose the administrator carefully. His or her skills will have to be broad and deep, and passion for the program is essential. It's better to hire a local person, if possible, because the community relationships that person brings and develops are paramount.

Starting a crisis center is a huge undertaking. However, before dismissing the idea, contact—or better yet visit—a successful one.[54]

Alternative Mobile Crisis Center Unit

A more realistic alternative to a 24/7 free-standing crisis center is a mobile crisis unit. This idea is guided by a Memorandum of Understanding (MOU) between law enforcement and mental health service providers who are willing to participate. Likewise, a mental health emergency department at a hospital works well when there's a documented understanding of duties and responsibilities. (Appendix: CIT Mobile Crisis Management Fact Sheet.)

More than likely, initial crisis response will be a combination of response alternatives and resources. For example, there may be a local detox center that can assume custody. The goal for crisis response is an expeditious and routine transfer of custody.

For a mobile team, the goal is a 20-minute response, which has proven to be quite realistic. This is especially true when the MOU establishes the criteria for dispatch by the 911 telecommunicator or the telecommunicator has a police radio.

Mobile crisis response works best when officers have a place to take the consumer, such as—and preferably—a 24/7 facility. If part of the crisis accommodation involves a hospital, an MOU covering drop-off responsibilities is necessary. If the accompanying officer is inordinately delayed at the hospital while transferring custody, that alternative won't work. In that scenario, the CIT officer is compelled to consider arrest even if reluctant to do so.

One example of a creative answer to crisis response came from a mental health catchment area in North Carolina: The psychiatric ward at the local hospital agreed to assume custody of a consumer in crisis. Another area established a helpline for CIT officers and the mobile crisis team. Where there's a will, there are ways of steering a consumer to qualified mental health professionals and away from courts and correction, while keeping the officer in the community.

According to CIT officials, mental health response and referral require systems and policy statements that give law enforcement real alternatives. According to a crisis center director, "Mental health has to change to make CIT work; CIT has to make sense for law enforcement supervisors to send officers to training and for officers to see that training translates to real benefit."

Map Local Services and Create a Common Playbook

Whatever the accommodation, it will take active management and persistence to work out the kinks. Then you'll need a thorough understanding of services and a concise listing of them.

Effective Practice

Map local services that are alternatives to arrest for law enforcement.

Assessing community services to prevent incarceration requires extensive research and analysis. You'll need to list what services are available and determine how those services can be employed in the work of diversion. A necessary task, filling gaps in available services is a job separate from implementing and stabilizing CIT. Mapping resources for CIT and how to access them involves listing them in a brochure or cataloguing them, preferably in a resources binder for easy reference for the responding officer. Once the cataloguing of services is done, the binder is a convenient "action" manual as it can be the repository for checklists, references, and pertinent information. Plus, it's easy to update, which people will want to do regularly. Using the same playbook facilitates collaboration among all CIT players.

Once you've created a brochure or assembled a binder, distribute it beyond CIT officers. It needs to be available to everyone concerned with the chain of events leading up to a crisis event and including incarceration. Why? Because multiple opportunities arise to divert a consumer, from a criminal justice response to a call for service. Many individuals with mental illness have a brush with law enforcement, courts, and corrections for a misdemeanor, for which myriad alternatives are available. Many times, the solution is as simple as taking the consumer to a family member. This person can then help the consumer reconnect with his or her established network of providers and community supports and receive care, therapy, and perhaps medication. Again, the process begins with surveying your local services and mapping where they are.

Following is a diversion story involving a minor infraction. It was adapted from an article introducing the VITALS app, a helpful mental health tool in the diversion process.[55]

A Case of Luck – The Need for CIT

Driving down a neighborhood street during the day, an officer came across a boy who appeared to be in seventh or eighth-grade. Out walking his dog, the boy was standing on the sidewalk urinating.

When the officer approached the boy and tried to interact with him, he quickly realized the young man had some sort of disability or vulnerability.

He probably wasn't dangerous or violent or at risk of hurting himself or anybody else, but the officer and his partner couldn't just drive away and let it go.

The officers decided to try to guide the young man to the squad car and attempt to take him home.

As they were working on this endeavor, a car stopped, and it was a teacher from the local school. He recognized the boy and called him by name. The young man responded to the teacher because he knew him.

But the situation wasn't necessarily resolved.

About a week later, the boy's mother sent an email to the chief of police asking what would have happened if that teacher hadn't driven by.

The chief, without CIT training, didn't have a good answer for her. The situation could have gone several different ways, depending on a variety of factors.

People with mental illness and other disabilities or conditions that affect their ability to communicate or behave in accordance with social norms are at risk in encounters with community members and law enforcement. Not only that, but the officers involved are at a disadvantage.

Had the officers been CIT trained, they would have had the skills to begin a connection with the boy and mental health resources to call for appropriate assistance.

Capacity Assessment Roundtable

A good place to start assessment of your resources is by assembling CIT stakeholders for a capacity assessment roundtable,[56] or an action team if you prefer. Primary responsibility for the survey and assembling resources falls to mental health professionals at the LME. Assessing municipal services is already part of what they do so they have a head start.

The object is to specify where in the community these services are located and how to contact them—even in the middle of the night, if necessary, when staff may be gone. Obviously, the responding officer will be most interested in services in or nearest his or her beat.

Your capacity assessment group can begin by listing resources and services they know exist. The Five County Mental Health Authority suggests considering the following networks:

- Adult mental health services
- Juvenile mental health services
- Adult developmental disability services
- Juvenile developmental disability services
- Adult day health
- Crisis respite
- Enhanced respite
- Crisis services

- Day support
- Enhanced personal care
- Personal care services
- Home and community supports
- Home supports
- Individual care-giving training and education
- Long-term vocational supports
- Residential supports
- Respite care
- Respite care, non-institutional nursing based
- Specialized consultative services
- Supported employment
- Substance abuse services (adult and child/adolescent)
- Private transportation services

This list suggests how you can organize the binder. Tab your binder per your list for easy reference and immediate action when needed. Implied is an understanding of how to make access to these services realistic and helpful.

CIT officials also recommend asking the following service providers if they can add to the CIT resources reference binder:

- School resource officers and their assigned school(s)
- Magistrates
- Corrections officials, especially jail officials
- 911 telecommunicators
- Assigned state highway patrol officers
- Private law enforcement officers who may be assigned to a hospital or a university

Keep in mind that service capacity means *a consumer must be able to access those mental health services,* according to a NAMI representative. When a service capability is logged, determine its:

- *Depth* – How many providers exist for each category?
- *Access* – Can the consumer get to or be carried to the service?

- *Affordability* – Does the service offer viable payment options for the consumer?
- *Adequacy* – Is the service provider competent?

You'll need to inform the services network about CIT and how each provider fits into the scheme of diversion.

In the case of CIT, realistic access to services is determined by the type of consumer, who is accompanied by the law enforcement officer responding. Keep it simple. The goal is a practical services resource/reference manual. Separate this task from the much more detailed and separate work of determining a *complete* array of municipal services, attained by adding missing mental health services over time. Remember, the focus of CIT is *diversion from jail.* All else derives from that.

Addressing the Issues of Time and People Power

Previously, we addressed creating your vision, mission, and goals, which define the parameters of your program. A major theme when beginning a CIT program is simplicity. Keep your program scope a matter of doing only the essentials and doing them well—not necessarily because money is limited, but because *people power is.* Capacity Building is the work of assembling and developing social capital: The whole becomes much greater than the sum of its parts. Some rationalize that "CIT can be done on a shoestring" or "We aren't spending any big money, so we won't go over budget." True, funding is always a sticky issue, but CIT is not as concerned with financial issues as other programs. Why not? Because instructors are volunteers; training facilities can be made available gratis via technical colleges and state supported classes; students attend classes as part of the duty day; and advocates volunteer for anything else necessary to train a critical mass of people.

Time – The Most Serious Restriction

The real restriction on the program is people's time to get the work done. The individuals involved with CIT are some of the busiest people in public service, so the program must economize their time. A CIT coordinator in a sheriff's office lamented that she's the only one in a large office to coordinate the program, and she does it part-time. Her CIT duties could occupy a full-time officer, but that's not in the budget. It's tough to find a qualified, "inspired" coordinator. Funding staff is a sticky wicket. If this coordinator were to take on the job full time, the sheriff's office might lose the support of soft grant money for her part-time position.

Next, let's move on to consider the process of determining if your program is running well and achieving its stated goals.

The individuals involved with CIT are some of the busiest people in public service, so the program has to economize their time.

Designing Impact Analysis

Data gathering is the first thing abandoned or not done well during program development. During the workday, much clamors for attention, and gathering numbers is pesky busywork for many people. Yet collecting data is the most productive task program stakeholders can do. If you keep the numbers simple and make sure they're understood and used correctly to justify the program, your operations will be efficient and effective. You'll also have a better chance of institutionalizing the idea in the community. Be *encouraged* by the prospects of doing a little number crunching.

Initial CIT data can be used to:

- *Analyze impact* – Communities can see the impact diversions have on their neighborhoods.
- *Justify court proceedings* – The criminal justice system can justify taking a consumer to court, *if need be,* according to a senior sheriff's office CIT coordinator. Make the case with the numbers and examples that it's good business.
- *Make budgetary decisions* – Municipalities are more likely to support the program if shown that diversion saves incarceration costs. Cost saving appeals to the stakeholders in the criminal justice community and to taxpayers. It's highly cost-effective to divert.
- *Strengthen the CIT effort* – Good data indicating progress strengthens the CIT effort, which serves mental health stakeholders and advocates. More benefits accrue to the municipality and taxpayers.
- Prove the program's effectiveness – Most important, citizens are served by an efficient, effective public service. Data shows that communities see fewer and fewer consumer arrests as CIT programs mature.

... Collecting data is the most productive task program stakeholders can do.

- *Make the case for CIT in other locales* – Data can provide compelling economic justification for replication, needed staffing, additional services, and resource reallocation. Data helps justify the critical need for crisis response.

- *Guide program conduct and expansion* – CIT data provides the basis for course-to-course training modifications, community public relations, and the evolution of the vision to decriminalize people living with mental illness. Data will eventually make CIT a sterling household name, according to a NAMI senior official.

"As a police lieutenant who implemented a Crisis Intervention Team, or CIT Program, within my police department, I can honestly tell you that CIT saves lives and taxpayer dollars and diverts many citizens in need of mental health treatment to appropriate services, away from the costly and many times inappropriate criminal justice system."
– Christopher Hoina, Sr., Lt., Retired;
Cary, North Carolina, Police Department

Effective Practice

Map local services that are alternatives to arrest for law enforcement.

Costs of Arrest

The costs of housing and treating a consumer in the criminal justice system continue to escalate, according to a founding member of the North Carolina CIT initiative. The burden of these costs, however, is only part of the story. The funds that go to treating consumers in de facto mental health hospitals, i.e., jails, are spent in lieu of developing community-based services that are far more efficient and effective for returning a consumer to social functionality.

In defense of your CIT program, research the following data points and compute the specific costs of arresting and incarcerating a consumer using the following computational description. This is your cost-effectiveness statement:

- *The cost of the average man hours to the criminal justice system* – This should be a conservative computation of average man hours spent by all the criminal justice professionals who process an arrestee during a typical path to a jail cell. This cost accrues before the costs of housing and treating a consumer are incurred.

- *Plus the marginal expense of keeping a consumer versus a "typical" inmate* - This may vary from jail to jail, but it's significant. Treating a consumer in jail is considerably more expensive than treating inmates without mental health complications.
- *Plus the cost of the increase in length of stay in jail* - Mentally ill inmates are usually incarcerated longer than other inmates.
- *Times the (conservative) number of diversions* - This data can be gathered by the responding officer, who will have criteria for determining what circumstances define a diversion.
- Equals the total cost of incarcerating a consumer that's saved and more efficiently allocated by the CIT effort.

The costs of an arrest times the number of diversions are the costs of arrests that have been avoided. This is the cost-effectiveness statement needed to justify CIT and additional resources. Run the data points through a pen-and-paper exercise if you wish; it's illuminating. Keep running totals so you can update promotional material, motivate staff, and above all, be ready to justify your budget. You can speak in terms of money saved—that CIT actually "makes" money rather than costs money. And that savings can be used to strengthen and expand services.

. . . CIT actually "makes" money rather than costs money.

By multiplying the total cost of an arrest and criminal justice involvement times the number of diversions, you get a whopping amount of money saved for the community.

Point out that jail for those needing mental health services is shockingly more expensive than delivering those services in the community with local resources. Plus, using jail as the de facto mental health hospital is a gross misappropriation of limited resources—not to mention a disservice to people living with mental illness who haven't committed crimes that call for incarceration.

Savings and Tradeoffs

Err on the side of simplicity because this cost-effectiveness calculation will have to be updated from time to time. A running update is best and can be used for progress to goal accomplishment. Estimation is expected and suffices for bolstering the CIT position. Be conservative with your estimates and include explanations for how the final number was derived. The number will be compelling, but it will be only part of the debate. Tell your story; use examples and narratives of successful diversions; get testimonials to highlight the budget request.

Beyond the dollars-and-cents debate is the broader view of treating our less fortunate neighbors as just that—*our neighbors.*

You'll probably receive counter-arguments to your cost-effectiveness statement. The most obvious will likely be something along the lines of: "But the costs of serving mental health consumers are still borne by our social institutions and our community." True! But the community represents public, private, and private nonprofit social networks and services that can deliver services for the people living with mental illness more efficiently and effectively than the criminal justice system. Also, neighbors and families in the community can care for a consumer, but not so when they're incarcerated. The community can muster many more appropriate, accessible, and economic options than incarceration.

Make the point that community services are much better equipped to handle a misdemeanant than the criminal justice system. Also point out that many diversions are "no cost." For example, a CIT officer may deliver a consumer to their Uncle Joe, who can get his niece back on her medications and to her physician or psychologist.

Beyond the dollars-and-cents debate is the broader view of treating our less fortunate neighbors as just that—*our neighbors.*

Finish the data-based argument with a statement about tradeoffs: Delineate services being sacrificed to jail a consumer that become possible with CIT savings. For example, CIT-husbanded resources may go to gang and delinquency prevention, reentry aftercare, out-of-school programming, or counseling for child victims of domestic violence. You'll find many examples relevant to your locale and dear to your main (budgetary) decision makers.

These points based on costs and savings will be the core of your argument for and justification of your program throughout the duration of a CIT program in your town. This argument is relatively simple to devise and portray (e.g., presented in a one-page fact sheet) and easy to understand. Once the system of data collection and reporting is in place, it becomes relatively quick, easy, and efficient. More important, it becomes part of the daily routine, with growing help for getting the numbers together, especially when you gain program support.

Next, we'll consider a few essential measures to determine how well your CIT program is doing.

Analyzing and Measuring Progress

When considering what to analyze, go back to your mission: decriminalizing the mental health consumer via jail diversion to contribute to community well-being. The data you collect needs to flow from that. When you collect data, keep in mind that less is more. Every variable you consider increases the complexity and sophistication required to collect, analyze, and especially report findings. More data becomes confusing, requires more staff capacity, and distracts the program from its basic purposes. Data is a best friend and can become insidious in that every piece of data that's "nice to have" leads to another and another that's equally "nice to have" or even considered "essential." Soon the vitality and purpose of the data disappear, staff waste valuable time, and worse yet, the program derails—sometimes fatally.

Ideally, focus on one or two "golden" measures that are vital to assessing the accomplishment of your stated goals. Always ask, "How will this information be used?" If you struggle to determine its use, ax it summarily. Then make sure you use the information assessed as defined.

Effective Practice

Map local services that are alternatives to arrest for law enforcement.

Tailoring Data to Stakeholder Interests

Initial measures should focus on law enforcement needs for performance, which is a public safety measurement. CIT is an essential and important preventive policing tool, much preferred to arrest. Data must indicate and highlight the CIT alternative because it reduces arrests. This information is important to all stakeholders but first to sheriffs and police. It's a quadruple public sector win: Law enforcement wins, the mental health consumer wins, the community wins, and the criminal justice system wins.

When the program is established and policing data is effectively being gathered and used for program justification and management, *then* consider adding variables. For example, a sheriff, a police chief, and a judge would be interested in community safety and thus interested in decreasing rearrest and injury rates after they see arrests steadily decrease. Each of the following measures can be used to address the concerns of key stakeholders.[57]

- *Diversions* – If you can afford to focus only on tallying diversions from the criminal justice system, that would be enough. Diversions are basic to determining overall program impact in monetary terms. A corollary of this measure would be to filter out the number of misdemeanants diverted. This makes a compelling emotional and cost-effective statement to decision makers and especially budgetary officials. Always explain the tradeoffs.
- *Injuries* – Reduction in officer and civilian injuries concerns every stakeholder.
- *Time efficiency* – CIT means responding officers will spend much less time on a call and thus will be able to return to primary duties more quickly. Time spent could be a matter of minutes, whereas previously they would spend hours—or simply make a convenient arrest because they had no alternatives.
- *Effectiveness* – Dispatching a trained CIT officer sets off a positive chain of events that conserves the limited resources of the criminal justice system. Rather, it uses community-based resources that specialize in the needs of consumers—a much more efficient and effective allocation of limited and dear resources. Remember that every dollar of taxpayers' money spent is not a pure and simple transaction; it comes at the expense of doing something else that's equally or more important.

After the program has experienced success, consider collecting additional information,[58] but keep the previously mentioned cautions in mind. You might collect data on:

- *CIT calls for service to law enforcement* – This monitors demands on CIT stakeholders and resources.
- *Calls for transportation/referral* – This also monitors demands on limited law enforcement CIT-trained officers and staff.
- *Post-booking diversions* – You may find it helpful to monitor any diversions from jail to a mental health court. This is another factor contributing to the cost-efficiency argument to justify your diversion program.
- *Expansion* – It's helpful to monitor when CIT training expands to other first responders, stakeholders, and individuals in the community. More

people trained means more and more efficiencies and overall positive effects on individuals, agencies, and neighborhoods.

- *Mental health crisis facility admissions* – These numbers inform stakeholders of the use and distribution of resources.
- *Hospital psychiatric inpatient admissions and total days in treatment* – This is yet another mark of appropriate use of resources. Otherwise, the public sector local jail must take on the financial, procedural, and processing burden of treatment during consumer incarceration.
- *Substance abuse crisis facility admissions* – These numbers indicate further appropriate use of resources that keeps services in the community and usually with the private sector.
- *Involuntary treatment costs* – Again, appropriate use of resources. These costs would otherwise be borne by the criminal justice system as jail would act as the default mental health hospital.
- *Strength of collaborative efforts* – This data helps tell the story of how well a CIT program is working and where more needs to be done or resources need to be reappropriated.

Notice how these items largely measure efficiencies that can be monetized. Each contributes to making the argument that CIT is the smart thing to do for the municipality and its citizens.

Creating Reports

Whatever you do, don't sit on your data once you've compiled it.[59] Properly done, analysis provides constant feedback on progress or the lack thereof. Compiling data "makes goals happen," according to a CIT coordinator for a North Carolina sheriff. The coordinator also commented that wise use of this data "sustains interest" that compels buy-in.

Create your reports to appeal to your target audiences. A simple fact sheet is most effective. Work in the public sector is demanding, and public professionals don't have time to read long, sometimes tedious reports that don't hit the mark. A fact sheet with a chart makes their job easier and helps them remember your case. It can support appeals for assistance, public relations, and program credibility. A small flyer may be all that's necessary to make the case for funding CIT coordinators, a mental health court, and jail diversion to round out cost-effective diversion services. It can also be handy when addressing community groups. Information dovetails well with developing the relationships necessary for all-important political and tangible support, especially funding.

Nurturing Relationships

A CIT program isn't reaching its potential until the entire cadre of possible first responders and need-to-know citizens are trained or exposed to it. CIT coordinators must be in the sheriff's office or report to the sheriff, and in police departments and the LMEs. One sheriff who understands the impact of CIT has a goal of having his department 100 percent trained in CIT, whether through full or abbreviated classes. Training can then expand to all emergency responders.

Anticipate inevitable turnover. You can offer refresher courses when the primary training is completed and overview courses for community leadership, management, and the citizenry. CIT needs to continue as long as decriminalizing the people living with mental illness remains a concern.

As previously suggested, any expenses of offering the first class can often be shared. Compared to the costs of implementing other local programs such as an anti-gang initiative or a neighborhood renewal program, CIT costs can be quite bearable. Again, it depends on your unique situation and how you structure your program.

It's essential to nurture relationships with a range of stakeholders. It helps to understand the jurisdictional characteristics of each of the primary stakeholders, beginning with law enforcement.[60] Develop a thorough understanding of stakeholder agency resources. Become familiar with their relevant rules, policies, regulations, laws, and standard operating procedures. Attend their meetings. Attend official functions. Attend what is appropriate and important to them. You're developing allies and, especially, lasting friends.

You can offer refresher courses when the primary training is completed and overview courses for community leadership, management, and the citizenry.

Work to understand the various styles of leaders you want to buy into CIT. Will a police chief, for example, want to have his or her CIT officers fully trained or simply trained in de-escalation techniques? Will a sheriff insist on an ironclad agreement for emergency response and consumer hand-off arrangements within a certain amount of time?

Also become familiar with the local mental health system that will be essential in responding to consumer needs. If the program is in a rural jurisdiction, will it need a reciprocal agreement with neighboring municipalities for training or services? This is all part of developing the necessary relationships that undergird successful CIT programs. It's essential Capacity Building.

Effective Practice

Map local services that are alternatives to arrest for law enforcement.

Before the first class of students sits, your program poison is passivity—the real threat of inertia. The antidote to it is networking. At this stage of planning, you have the essentials of relationship building in place. The planning group and teams know their roles. They understand their capacity (resource) needs. Vision and mission are tailored to the locality and can be articulated for specific audiences. The teams can address the economic sense of CIT and have measures that are meaningful to the needs of primary partners. In other words, they are prepared to promote the CIT message wherever and whenever needed.

A successful mental health representative suggests the following list of potential supporters of—or those in need of—the CIT program. Some have been mentioned already or are obvious; others are new:

- *Law enforcement entities* – This category extends to the many private sworn entities at our hospitals, universities, and malls, for example.
- *Mental health entities* – These resources are part of the network of alternatives to incarceration.
- *Elected officials* – See your mayor, council members, judges, and district attorneys early and often. They can make your CIT effort—or break it, if they're uninformed about what it is and how it works. For example, an attempt to scale a remarkable reentry program was shot down by a town council member who had *never* visited the flagship service, a wildly successful *national* model.
- *Key public sector decision makers* – It's especially helpful to establish a solid working relationship with the town/county manager, for example.

- *Local businesses* – Businesspeople are most interested in CIT because a consumer in crisis in or near a place of business is quite disruptive and needs trained help.
- *The local health department* – This is a valuable community-based resource with sympathetic purposes.
- *The local Department of Social Services* – DSS is another valuable community-based resource with sympathetic interests.
- *Schools* – Schools aren't immune to mental health crises, and they may not be staffed to handle them.
- *Media* – A forward-thinking law enforcement executive suggests meeting with the media early on, before an unfortunate incident or crisis occurs. Let these people know they'll be informed of newsworthy events and establish the expectation that any media coverage will be collegial. Be prepared with a press kit for the CIT message and statement that compels action and support. Again, this can be as simple as a fact sheet.
- *Community social organizations* – Make sure a member of the CIT collaborative is invited to the regular meetings of selected social organizations such as Kiwanis or the Shriners. They're remarkable community benefactors and their networks are spectacular.
- *Private foundations* – The United Way, for example, is always looking for successful community collaboratives.
- *The community at large* – Staff for one CIT program conducted mobile crisis information sessions at a National Night Out.

Effective Practice

Map local services that are alternatives to arrest for law enforcement.

Relationship building is a marketing strategy—not a part-time occupation or one-time shot. To be productive, it must continue as long as CIT exists, involving and starting with the key stakeholders. Even during planning, stakeholders can write articles for the local newspaper, put out flyers, or present to other stakeholders.

You'll want to make multiple contacts with target audiences and partners. Staff at one of the original CIT sites in North Carolina developed a multi-pronged marketing strategy that still endures, with a few modifications. They shared these ideas:

- *The Road Show* – The state-level mental health representative developed a ready-for-the-road slide presentation that addresses how all stakeholders are winners with CIT. Many of the staff are trained to deliver it at a moment's notice.
- *Conference presentations* – Stakeholders offered to moderate panels or run workshops with the theme of CIT successes.
- *Training* – Staff took abbreviated CIT training to regional audiences.
- *Reaching out* – Formally and informally, they let any and all municipal officials who were interested or should be interested know about CIT. A professionally designed website helps.
- *Phone campaigning* – They campaigned for CIT by phone, assisted by NAMI volunteers.
- *Video* – They even created a professional CIT video, which greatly widened viewing audiences.
- *Media* – Another suggestion is to employ social media. Consider putting a 20-something in charge; Boomers will likely understand why. As previously suggested, court local news outlets and reporters.

Your CIT group's marketing/relationship-building campaign is limited only by its degree of creativity, desire, and available time.

These original CIT champions saw themselves as mini-ambassadors, who made it a point to unabashedly promote CIT. Their CIT graduations, for example, are colossal celebrations extended to the mayor, legislators, commissioners, judges and magistrates, district attorneys, town managers, court counselors, 911 technicians, school resource officers, service providers and—of course—students and families. Not surprising, few of these people, who are usually "too busy" for such "frivolities," miss the chance to come. The festivities are conducted in conjunction with the county commissioner's meeting, where they also celebrate a decline in arrest rates. In addition, selected attendees get to "pin" each graduate with a CIT lapel pin. It's a genuinely good time with a resounding message of contribution, cooperation, collaboration, competency, and significance.

> "Relationships are based on reputation" and reputation is largely a face-to-face process, according to a CIT official. Each success enjoyed by CIT is the building block for the next accomplishment. Make friends early and often. "Connections are key," according to a founding LME CIT coordinator.

Developing Performance-Oriented Services for Consumers

The key to CIT service delivery is the training, but resist the temptation to dive right into doing the first class. First, while planning, make sure the critical tasks of developing leadership, determining scope (vision, mission, goals), assessing capacity, and building relationships are solidly underway and analysis and evaluation are readied for implementation. Then your training will be guided by your:

- *Vision* – Establishing a permanent CIT program that decriminalizes people living with mental illness and contributes to community well-being, with a municipal-wide reentry strategy. (See also Volumes III and IV in the Capacity Building Series: *Accelerating Juvenile Reentry and Accelerating Adult Reentry.*)
- *Mission* – Diverting consumers from the criminal justice system (jail) to appropriate care services.
- *Main Goal* – Making a marked, positive difference in community safety and well-being.

Effective, Efficient Diversion

Training won't be complete until you resolve how the call for service will be handled from the perspective of beat officers. They will be concerned with how quickly they'll be able to return to their beat. Therefore, CIT training will focus on de-escalation skills, law, and the most expeditious way to address the needs of the consumer. Arrest is a last resort.

The corollary to that is detailing how the response to the urgent/emergent situation will be handled. While law enforcement doesn't have responsibility for mental health services, awareness of those services and how to access them are critical to a successful diversion. Therefore, the CIT Program planning and implementation team turns to the mental health founding stakeholder to detail how the community is equipped to provide these services. Following is a list created by the North Carolina Five County Mental Health Authority of supports or services that may be involved with CIT responses. You'll need to get more specific for your area and detail where, when, and how supports and services can be implemented.

While law enforcement doesn't have responsibility for mental health services, awareness of those services and how to access them are critical to a successful diversion.

- *Natural supports* – Naturally occurring social supports, mainly family, for a consumer in crisis are the first consideration for a diversion.
- *Law enforcement* – CIT officers are an integral part of the comprehensive response.
- *Mobile crisis response* – For a successful CIT call, the responding officer must have mental health professionals readily available. If need be, the professional may even respond to the call for CIT service with the officer. This strength (and expertise) in numbers is ideal, especially for the consumer.
- *First responders beyond law enforcement* – These are the best equipped professionals other than trained CIT sworn officers and mental health professionals. An example is CIT-trained EMTs.
- *Mobile crisis team screening, triage, and referral* – Such are the first duties of the mobile crisis team, which becomes a portal to individual patient-specific services.
- *Developmental disabilities crisis response* – Many times, consumers have complicating developmental needs separate and different from mental health needs. It would be most helpful if these specialized services were also available. Discuss this with your CIT team to know what these needs are and how best to satisfy them.
- *Rapid response clinic* – This is a transitional service between hospital discharge and treatment with community-based services.
- *Recovery response services* – These services become necessary when first response requires a commitment to the hospital and community services don't work.

- *Hospital ERs and their mental health liaison* – Emergency departments may be the only appropriate environment for some consumers.

The following story illustrates a creative solution to decriminalizing mental illness.[61]

Help for Katelyn and a Valuable Resource

On a holiday, a double fatal car crash occurred on a rural county road. Officers blocked off a large area and squad car lights were flashing. An officer was directing traffic, standing guard so no one would drive around the barricades. A woman approached in a car and said, "I need to go that way."

"I'm sorry, ma'am," the officer replied, "but this road is closed."

The woman turned around and parked, which seemed odd to the officer. He radioed the sheriff's office patrol to explain the woman's actions, thinking she may be impaired by drugs or alcohol.

In this case, the deputy had a resource available to him that allowed him to act. When he arrived, a mental health app alerted him that he was within 80 feet of Katelyn, who lived with her parents and had a mild cognitive disability. Thus he was able to address Katelyn by name as he approached her.

When she asked how he knew who she was, the deputy explained he had an app that told him about her and asked if she was lost.

Katelyn replied, "Every Sunday, my parents allow me to drive to Walmart on this road to get a few things, and then I immediately come back." The blocked road was the only way she knew how to get home.

The deputy reassured Katelyn she was safe and he would get her home. With information from the app, he was able to call her worried parents, explain what had happened, and obtain their permission to escort her home via another route.

In this situation, the officer had to stay on duty. If CIT had been established in this community, the officer could have summoned a mental health practitioner for assistance. Fortunately, Katelyn's parents had set up the app to which the deputy had access and her condition was such that he could handle it. In many other cases, however, a deputy sheriff may not have the knowledge needed to help a mentally ill person. That said, your CIT team would likely find this app a useful resource. See CIT Program Resources and Key Contacts in the Appendix for information.

Encouraging Self-Management

Although mostly ignored, oftentimes, the consumer is capable of being accountable for his or her own condition and actions and should be encouraged to do so. Frequently, consumers state they just need understanding and an occasional hand. A firm but reassuring push, if you will, back to productivity, back to home, back to dignity. With this in mind, part of the CIT role is to facilitate consumers' self-management.[62] The overall goal is to facilitate a smooth, sustained, successful reentry into the community. Anyone who recidivates back into the criminal justice system is a disappointment in many ways. A win–win–win possibility becomes a lose–lose–lose reality.

Thus, training needs to emphasize consumer self-management, and CIT responders will want to encourage consumers to:

- *Be aware* of their rights.
- *Take part* in making decisions for their well-being. For example, ask if they have a Wellness Recovery Action Plan (WRAP),[63] a Psychiatric Advance Directive (PAD),[64] a VITALS app,[65] or even a peer they go to for support.
- *Improve* their quality of life and focus on a recovery-oriented approach.
- *Develop* a positive sense of self with purpose and meaning.
- *Connect* with community social networks.
- *Communicate* with anyone who can support their wellness (health) and well-being (state of mind).

Developing Training to Fit Officers and Consumers

When you train beat officers, be aware that training is a mix of what the officer needs, such as legal considerations, and what the consumer needs, such as de-escalation.

Effective Practice

Design CIT training to fit both law enforcement and the mental health consumer.

"All law enforcement personnel who respond to incidents in which an individual's mental illness appears to be a factor receive training to prepare for these encounters; those in specialized assignments receive more comprehensive training. Dispatchers, call takers, and other individuals in a support role receive training tailored to consumer needs.[66]

Full CIT training in North Carolina is a 40-hour course and involves a combination of gaining knowledge and skills and learning regulations/law. (See the Appendix: CIT 40-Hour Course Schedule Sample.)

Classes need to be highly professional in preparation, production, and presentation. They must also be effective from a law enforcement perspective as officers will be receiving educational credit. The training and certification may be used as part of departmental accreditation, a big draw for law enforcement partners.

An important feature of the basic class is that it evolves with the needs of the community and the attendees according to the staff who teach the various topics. As an overview, the major topics consist of the following:[67]

- *Public safety law* and the CIT call for service
  - What is CIT?
  - Legal aspects, policies and procedures, and mental consumer commitment law
  - CIT data collection
  - De-escalation skills and crisis intervention/active listening (role modeling)
  - Using less lethal weapons and alternatives to use of force
  - Consumer resources
  - Local mental health crisis response orientation
- *Understanding mental illness* – Recognizing and assessing a person in crisis
  - What is mental illness?
  - Psychotropic medications and side effects
  - Substance abuse and co-occurring disorders
  - Special concerns with adolescents
  - Mental retardation, developmental disabilities, and autism
  - Personality disorders
  - Suicide risk assessment and intervention

The training and certification may be used as part of departmental accreditation, a big draw for law enforcement partners.

    - The homeless population and mental illness
    - Special concerns with geriatrics
    - Trauma/PTSD
- *Practical applications* – Experiencing consumers face to face as citizens and neighbors
    - Field visits
    - Consumer panel and family perspectives from consumer family participants
- *Graduation ceremonies* – Celebrating in grand style, with a who's who list of attendees

Training Hierarchy

Your hierarchy for training is to train sworn officers first and non-sworn personnel second; and then offer awareness classes to your widening spheres of interested people and groups. Training is never complete until all need-to-know people have been trained or exposed to CIT. The idea is to get your patrol force trained in numbers enough to cover each shift with CIT qualified officers. Then modify the training to cover the next layer of need-to-know staff, for example, telecommunicators, Emergency Medical Services (EMS) personnel, magistrates, and jail staff. Awareness classes can be offered to reentry staff, pre-trial release staff, probation staff, judges, and elected officials—and don't forget John Q. Public. Your ever-widening contacts also become some of your best cheerleaders and salespeople; train them and entrust them with these functions.

Training Tips

You're well advised to have select students, such as 911 operators, help design their own course. That way, it will cover what they need to know for their position.

Another helpful—no, mandatory—tool is an end-of-course critique. (See the Appendix: CIT Pre/Post-Training Questionnaire.) The critique can consist of a few simple questions to cover how instructors performed, how appropriate the topics were, what went well, and what needs improvement. When you ask participants to provide feedback, be sure to use their responses to improve your training. Don't fail to take advantage of this opportunity. And if a student provides contact information, send a note or make a call of thanks, especially if you used a suggestion offered. Ask and they will tell; take the inevitably good hints and act on them.

By progressing through the life cycle of planning your CIT program and getting ready for your first class, you will have addressed most, but not all, of your staffing issues. As you hire and develop your staff, encourage them to internalize how their performance specifically and individually contributes to decriminalizing the people living with mental illness and helps with community well-being.

Developing Staff for Performance and Team Effort

Human capacity development for CIT is less complex than other service programs in which staff must be developed from pre-hire to post-retirement. Staff are considered those who support the program but aren't involved in response to calls for service. Essentially, they're CIT coordinators and classroom instructors/facilitators.

When you ask participants to provide feedback, be sure to use their responses to improve your training.

CIT Coordinators

Most important to the initial stability and necessary permanence of your CIT program are the CIT coordinators in the law enforcement entities and LME. They are the bridge between CIT and stakeholders, particularly consumers and CIT officers.[68]

Your CIT coordinators must be facilitators—people ". . . who can identify leadership and build consensus among diverse groups (who then) undestand and achieve new solutions to old problems."[69] You can find this unique person within either the public, private, or private nonprofit sectors. He or she has a clear sense of how to build a diversion program, mixed with intense interest for the job. Most times, these people are "on a mission." They have intimate knowledge of how the criminal justice and mental health systems work, formally and informally. They're highly experienced and have the commensurate credibility to promote a new way of thinking and doing.[70] Their passion for and commitment to the CIT program as well as their skill and work ethic make them examples of values-driven leadership.

When you ask participants to provide feedback, be sure to use their responses to improve your training.

Effective Practice

Choose law enforcement-oriented CIT coordinators.

The CIT coordinator for a county or a catchment area of several counties is a full-time position. However, the coordinators at the law enforcement entities can begin part-time until duties demand full-time attention. Again, look to incrementalize all you do to avoid overstepping your resources or abilities. Overpromising and underdelivering are common if insidious perils.

Successful CIT coordinators offer these further suggestions of qualities and qualifications that enhance their chances of success. It helps if coordinators are:

- *Eager* – First, the sworn CIT coordinator must want the job.
- *Patient and calm* – The job requires a well-grounded person, realistic and resolute about how to get things done.
- *Well versed in CIT* – A coordinator must be trained and periodically refreshed in CIT processes and methods.
- *Excellent with communicating* – Strong, clear verbal, written, and electronic communications are paramount for interfacing with the many CIT stakeholders and the public. Ensure this person "speaks their language."
- *Experienced in law enforcement* – The law enforcement CIT coordinator needs to be familiar with law enforcement procedures and how the criminal justice system works in his or her locale. For example, no less than a sergeant in a sheriff's office should hold the position of CIT coordinator. A localized approach is important as every jurisdiction does things its own way.

The community-wide coordinator (from a North Carolina LME) needs to be:

- *Goal directed* – Success depends on setting and reaching goals, resolving barriers to goal accomplishment along the way.
- *Good at shepherding the various stakeholders* – He or she must keep the partnership together.
- *Flexible and forward-looking* – The coordinator must constantly integrate appropriate well-considered change.

- *Good at teaching and promoting* – He or she must conduct wide community orientation and outreach, which means audiences will differ, so approaches may need modifying.
- *Independent* – The coordinator needs to be an independent worker and thinker. Look for the self-starters.
- *Frugal* – This quality is necessary given the often-sparse monetary and human capital resources for CIT.
- *Calm* – The CIT coordinator must be calm in VUCA, as *volatility, uncertainty, chaos, and ambiguity* are common occurrences in life with CIT. The program aims to resolve management by crisis.
- *Excellent at multitasking* – This position requires juggling many balls and wearing many hats as aptly and comfortably as possible. This includes being a consensus builder, dispute resolver, and diplomat.

Don't worry, these people are out there. Most likely, they will find you as the passion and purpose of CIT spreads.

In addition, the LME CIT coordinator needs to have a healthy respect for and willingness to take direction from law enforcement. The position will likely involve reporting to the lead law enforcement officer, particularly the sheriff. According to a successful CIT coordinator, the job is one of being a good listener, team builder, and consensus maker, while representing the calm center of the storm.

Once that person is in place, he or she can continue professional CIT development with local training and state, national, and international conferences.

Remember, no matter how wonderful your coordinator is, it's smart to have a succession plan in place. In fact, make succession planning for key people a part of the planning process.

CIT Class Instructors

Next up, let's consider qualities and qualifications for your classroom instructors. These people are obviously integral to the program.

Effective Practice

Choose performance-oriented CIT class instructors.

Arriving at the right mix of instructors is an evolutionary process. Choose instructors who are concerned with their program effectiveness and the performance of their class members versus those who simply teach procedures. Naturally, they need to have CIT knowledge and teaching expertise with CIT experience. As important as their professional qualifications is their ability to connect to the officer on patrol. This takes concerted effort. A non-sworn person from the mental health field must identify with a sworn officer and the uniqueness of what officers do. Traditionally, this has been a tough bond to cement, yet it must be done. CIT officers perform by successfully diverting a consumer; thus instructors need to internalize how they contribute to this goal.

. . . Instructors can't be boring. An engaging personality and teaching style keep students awake, attuned to what's being said, and actively learning.

Class organizers at one successful CIT program rotated instructors until they had the right mix that communicated the mission, message, and means of CIT. Primarily, they chose instructors based on who connected with law enforcement students in the classroom and their organizational hierarchy, and what feedback they received on end-of-course critiques. According to one CIT coordinator, instructors can't be boring. An engaging personality and teaching style keep students awake, attuned to what's being said, and actively learning.

Course planners also reiterated the note of caution already mentioned: "Be ready for last-minute no-shows." Instructors are volunteers with demanding careers. While they have a real desire to be involved with CIT, they do have day jobs and will call in minutes before a scheduled class to say they must attend to pressing matters. This is VUCA in one of its brazen forms. Don't punt; be prepared.

Review

Now you've been methodically through the planning process. The first part of the life cycle is complete enough to conduct the first class (although planning is continuous, even continuously evolving). Core groups of law enforcement, mental health, and advocate professionals have come together in a networked matrix to address the difficulties of decriminalizing mental health consumers.

You have a strategic plan that crystallizes how you view pre-booking jail diversion. Capacity assessment has revealed available community-based services for diversion and resources to support CIT. A readiness scale has determined that it's time to implement the plan. (See the Appendix: CIT Program Readiness Checklist.) Operations will be guided by standard operating procedures or Memos of Understanding.

You've established a 24/7 crisis response arrangement that's satisfactory to law enforcement. Alternatives to arrest have been mapped and organized in a reference manual. The vision and mission are performance oriented and ready to guide daily decision making. The group understands the impact of CIT in terms of cost savings to jails and the tradeoff of not doing CIT. Limited but pertinent data supporting the program will be collected, analyzed, and reported, with focus on the cost-effectiveness/tradeoff arguments.

A network of friends of CIT are ready to lend support via expertise, political persuasion, hard resources, volunteering, or funding. The classroom experience addresses the needs of officers and consumers alike via professional presenters, and motivated trainees are scheduled. All are aware of how CIT contributes to reentry by reducing incarceration rates and recidivism.

This thorough planning equips staff with the knowledge, and especially the confidence, to solve problems. It answers most of the major difficulties of implementation that would stop a program before it becomes permanent, such as lack of support and a misunderstanding of purpose and scope. The program core group has worked up to the moment when the collective realization dawns that it's time to begin. Any ruminating on a few more odds and ends is not productive. Over-preparation, especially born of risk aversion, is the enemy of progress. Stakeholders are working and collaborating as a true matrix of problem solvers and change agents.

The time has come to put the action into your action plan!

"If you want happiness for an hour – take a nap. If you want happiness for a day – go fishing. If you want happiness for a month – get married. If you want happiness for a year – inherit a fortune. If you want happiness for a lifetime – help someone else."

– Chinese Proverb

Chapter 4

PHASE II. OPERATE AND STABILIZE

Chapter 4

PHASE II. OPERATE AND STABILIZE

Colorado Springs Community Response Team

"If you want to build a ship, don't drum up people together to collect wood and don't assign them tasks and work, but rather teach them to long for the endless immensity of the sea."
–Antoine de Saint-Exupéry

The time for thinking big is over. Visioning has long been accomplished. It's now time to act with deliberate confidence in the fashion, form, and function of this new way of building service capacity. But as contrary to that as it may sound, you need to first think small and doable. Incrementalize.

CIT operations begin when the date for the first class is scheduled. Remember: Successful implementation for CIT is bottom up. This means the community view of what's needed and how to satisfy those needs is critical, if not preeminent.[71] This is important because most public service programs are largely top down, which complicates the grassroots nature of successful ideas such as CIT. The idea of bottom up is a fundamental precept of 21st-century leadership.

A study of the Ohio CIT model determined implementation that works focuses on the dual problems of ensuring permanence and maintaining a viable partnership.[72] These issues are resolved when the community takes ownership for "their" CIT program and continuously works on maintaining the partnership of law enforcement and the community via outreach.[73]

Your operation becomes reality when it becomes part of your community as the tangible extension of planning. You've worked hard and the collective wisdom, a feeling, says enough is enough, planning is over, it's time. Throw any timid thoughts aside and *act*.

Making Daily Operations Work

An extensive study of the Georgia statewide CIT implementation process revealed that a successful jail diversion program is primarily a specialized police response and strategy.[74] The study also noted that the Georgia CIT operation has certain characteristics that define its success. It is:

- *Multidisciplined* – Despite its police base, it involves many disciplines.
- *Goal oriented* – Training is oriented toward achieving certain goals that eventually improve community well-being.
- *Role specific* – Coordinators have defined roles.
- *Consistent* – Regular, organized meetings are held.
- *Practical* – Operations have practical guidelines.
- *Community-based* – Services are based in the community.
- *Frugal* – Costs are minimalized, and funding is frugally managed.
- *Forward-looking* – The group plans expansion based on evaluation, research, and collaborations.

According to a founding sheriff's deputy CIT coordinator, operation of the CIT program is a task of "sitting on the nest." It requires attending to every *relevant* detail and maintaining *reasonable* vigilance. She also observed that operation implementation continues the "fun" of making a real difference. Notice this attitude—that doing something that seems just a bit out of reach of personal and collective capabilities, and perhaps a little scary, is actually exhilarating! People find they had the "right stuff" all along, and it feels good!

Gearing Leadership for Permanency

A primary task for leadership is keeping the coalition of key stakeholders together.[75] It's a bit like herding cats. The early champions are now faced with the unglamorous challenges of combining myriad details of people, resources, supplies, rules, and regulations, Memorandums of Understanding, schedules, instructors, and multiple agencies into a single-purposed entity. Many informal relationships are now formalized. Calls can be made directly to decision makers and people who will implement CIT. Relationship building is in full swing. The core leaders' joint role now matures from planner to advisor, or mentor if you will, to workers in the trenches delivering the planned services.

Effective Practice

Establish a CIT advisory board for oversight and necessary work.

The advisory board during implementation/operation may or may not be comprised of the original champions of the program, but hopefully most of them remain. Founders who prefer the creativity of shaping an idea to the duties of making it work may drift away. As much as possible, it's helpful to preserve an operational nucleus of partners. Shaped by the needs of CIT, they have more than a little stake in seeing their ideas realized and are willing to do the tough work of implementation. The board redirects its energies from fleshing out the concept to overseeing and perhaps even being involved in operations. They might jump in and teach a segment of the first class, for example.

The Georgia CIT advisory board has overall objectives that focus on individual rights and quality-of-life issues.[76] These objectives include:

- *Safety* – To train law enforcement officers to respond safely to persons in mental health crises
- *Personal rights* – To protect the rights of persons with mental illnesses and other brain disorders
- *Treatment* – To ensure that persons with mental illnesses and other brain disorders receive treatment in lieu of incarceration, when appropriate
- *Quality of life* – To improve the quality and quantity of mental health services

- *Adequate training* – To promote adequate training for criminal justice personnel involved in the processes and decisions concerning incarceration or diversion of those with mental illnesses, developmental disabilities, and addictive diseases

A major purpose for this CIT advisory group is to ensure community leaders continue to be vested in making neighborhoods safer and more secure by diverting appropriate consumers from the criminal justice system. For example, they work out procedural issues of how to transfer custody to the crisis response service. They're concerned with quality services and their efficient, effective delivery and the program's continual improvement, looking for systemic weaknesses then correcting them. Decisions are more mundane and low-level during operations. However, the program needs tactful guidance—sometimes minute by minute.

Outreach is active and continual. A schedule has been established of people to see, meetings to conduct, teaching to do, organizations to visit, and presentations to make. The advisors meet with all manner of people, from local and state elected officials to community leaders, consumers, and citizens. This group discovered it's a good idea to contact state-level associations that represent sheriffs, police chiefs, and county commissioners, for example.

Data in the form of student feedback may require changes in class offerings and procedures. Training demands constant attention as students, instructors, and stakeholders come and go and a landslide of suggestions leads to constant curriculum tweaking. The advisory board also digests data regarding diversions and perhaps the reduction in recidivism and disseminates it to appropriate stakeholders.

Regularly scheduled meetings of the functional committees occur, but perhaps less frequently than before the first class. Crisis response poses problems that will require consensus resolution quickly. CIT won't work until an expeditious transfer of the consumer to the appropriate service provider or caretaker happens.

All concerned never lose sight of the fact that decriminalizing the mental health consumer is a step, albeit a big step, in creating community well-being—a condition in which people can thrive. That their CIT program is a collaborative matrix, a bottom-up, communal, living, breathing organism. This is the real purpose of public services, especially at the municipal level. Good things happen when people work together, beyond cooperation on a program to collaboration on a community goal.

Strengthening Law Enforcement/Mental Health Collaboration

Arrangements for services from community-based alternatives to incarceration take time to become functional. This functionality is complicated by the requirements of attending to the needs of the consumer. A successful mental health services director offered experienced advice for operational leadership: "Change [your] mentality to realize things aren't perfect—and that's okay; just move on." The connection between law enforcement and mental health resources is fundamental to CIT success.

A healthy way of looking at the problems or surprises you're bound to encounter is to reverse your natural tendency to get upset and say: "The [instructor didn't show]—so let's see what surprisingly good can come from this!" Such an attitude reverses a negative reaction with its toxic hormonal dump to a positive mindset of problem-solving with its positive infusion of strengthening hormones. Further, you can look at problems as opportunities to grow and improve and be creative. This is not an idle suggestion; Do it enough and it becomes an automatic response to solving problems, big and small. Another good example of 21st-century leadership in action.

Effective Practice

Strengthen the CIT collaborative between law enforcement and mental health CIT coordinators.

Responsibilities of CIT Coordinators

The duties and responsibilities of agency coordinators begin where those of the advisory board leave off. Coordinators ideally work seamlessly with CIT leadership to carry out the details of training, crisis response, and connecting services to consumers.

For example, *law enforcement coordinators* schedule CIT classes and in-service training and help choose or approve the officers who will attend. They help with data collection from the field, resolve procedural differences, and interpret rules, regulations, and points of law for responding officers. They act as the CIT right hand for agency leadership. In particular, they act for the sheriff or the police chief to coordinate the needs of the agency and resolve mental health issues. Coordinators will also be involved in outreach, classroom training, program justification, and making recommendations for deploying CIT trained men and women.

The *mental health coordinators* will do much of the same, with an emphasis on services. In particular, the CIT coordinators will be involved in efforts to bring CIT to neighboring sheriffs' offices and police departments.

Both law enforcement and mental health coordinators will help make the case for CIT to any interested or need-to-know individual or agency.

How to start?

A good way to begin is to pilot a training class with one law enforcement agency.

Effective Practice

Pilot your first 40-hour CIT class with officers from one sheriff's office.

The initial CIT program in North Carolina did just that with heralded success. Again, the theme of thinking small is a good strategy. You can work out the grander issues of coordinating multiple agencies and multiple municipalities more efficiently if you start the inaugural class with the most amenable agency. Amenable means you have full and vocal support from leadership to be the pilot agency. The best situation is when the senior law enforcement executive simply states his organization *will have CIT.*

Remember: All activities must support Capacity Building for permanency.

Capacity Assessment to Continuously Build Diversion Capability

Capacity Building is now the foundation for accomplishing goals, establishing a permanent presence in the community, and becoming socially transformative. It involves turning data into justification for needed resources such as salaries for coordinators, attraction of appropriate instructors, and funds for promotional materials. It's the work of seeing people, services, politics, real support, and training come together to provide alternatives to incarceration. Capacity Building begins with understanding community-based services.

Effective Practice

Continuously build and rebuild your community-based resources.

Mental health service partners are tasked with continually being aware of what and where services are located and how best to access them. The original CIT program in North Carolina updates these services annually. They organize services by geographic location for the convenience of law enforcement referrals and disseminate the information on one laminated sheet for easy reference. The idea is to train and equip the responding officer as completely as possible to make appropriate decisions.

How these services operate and connect to consumers is further reinforced by site visits conducted as a routine part of basic CIT training. Naturally, as officers respond to consumer calls for service, they become more aware of the local array of services. They note their relevance to particular consumers and how to access them appropriately. Jail diversion practitioners learn what can and cannot be done in their localities. All of this better serves the client and the community.

More services are always needed, especially in rural areas, according to mental health officials. The more these alternatives to incarceration are accessed, the more gaps in service become apparent. Although the problem seems to grow, what's growing is simply *awareness* of the problem at hand. Because these services are usually more cost efficient than jail, it's possible to make the case for wider support to fill gaps.

Services follow good business practices, not the other way around.

Establishing CIT Stability

The matrix of law enforcement, mental health services, and advocates works to fill service needs while delivering CIT. Still, CIT is more than pre-booking diversion.

Effective Practice

Actively pursue your plan for CIT stability.

Stability means making the *business* of CIT permanent. This is much more fundamental and different than offering courses, having CIT qualified officers available 24/7, and establishing a crisis response team and process. Strong, long-lasting CIT program practitioners understand the difference between the business of CIT and the services of CIT. What's the distinction? Services follow good business practices, not the other way around.

Good Business Practices

To help stabilize CIT as a business:

- *Formalize leadership duties and responsibilities* and how they operate within the system.
- *Modify the strategic plan as needed* after testing it in real situations.
- *Refine crisis response* after testing it live.
- *Ensure vision and mission are interwoven* into daily work and decision making. This goes with goal-driven tasking and activities.
- *Continue to tailor and expand CIT trainings* given feedback from students and field performance.
- *Routinize marketing and relationship building* to gain buy-in from stakeholders and the community in general.
- *Support post-booking ideas incrementally* without losing the focus of CIT being *the* pre-booking diversion tool. Many options exist for diversion after booking beyond jail and mental health courts. Look at community corrections, for example. All these options will benefit from exposure to what CIT is doing and how it's done, especially when you make the case for diversion in dollars and cents. A leading advocate observed that the secret to CIT success is "willingness to share."
- *Set boundaries* for what the team does. For example: Set up CIT jurisdictions, write specific response protocols, establish consumer disposition options for call screeners, and specify responsibilities for crisis response.
- *Document and share results.* Know who your key constituents are. Ask them what's important to them concerning CIT; don't assume to know what measures resonate. Elected officials may be concerned with effect on risk and liability. Police officials may want to see reduction in the use of force or reductions in officer time spent with mental health neighbors. The community may want to know how well-being is enhanced. Always put your case in cost-effective/ tradeoff terms. CIT is good "business."

Remember that good Capacity Building stays on task by actions that are goal directed. Revisit this at regular meetings. It's easy to get to the end of a day quite tired from your labors and have done little that matters; you worked on the "emergency" of the moment at the expense of the essential. Insidiously, you are in the grip of crisis management; and there is *always* another crisis 'round the bend.

The Importance of Dispatchers/Call Screeners

Recipients of calls for service need training and criteria to assess when circumstances do *not* warrant the involvement of a CIT officer or the mobile crisis unit. That makes it easier to decide where to redirect the caller for appropriate services rather than dispatching an officer.

> Contrary to what may seem implied, a service call may be handled by any practitioner or combination of practitioners along the path of diversion or arrest. A dispatcher can divert. A CIT officer can divert. A mobile crisis team can divert with no law enforcement involvement.

One of the elegant characteristics of CIT is that decisions for the consumer can be made at any level at which training is provided. This is the best use of limited resources and also models how matrix governance can work.

Yes, a dispatcher can take a large role in decriminalizing the mental health consumer. Training dispatchers to properly divert consumers assists the delivery of comprehensive services. It also fits the vision and mission of CIT, which keeps processes and procedures simple and efficient while still being effective. That same call recipient takes notes on the nature of the call and its disposition for future analysis. This assists in determining training and resources needed and crisis responses. According to a highly experienced mental health services provider, "The challenge is doing too much and going insolvent." Less is more seems to have universal application.

Analyzing calls is only part of understanding scope and how and *how well* CIT is working. Use what you're learning. For example, make sure the county manager knows the challenges of delivering CIT and how additional resources will enhance community safety and security.

One of the elegant characteristics of CIT is that decisions for the consumer can be made at any level at which training is provided. This is the best use of limited resources and also models how matrix governance can work.

A big part of achieving improvements in overall well-being is personal responsibility and accountability on the part of those living with mental illness and their families. However, they need to have services that will aid in developing that accountability.

Evolving Scope with Demand

One of the challenges of building CIT is to know the community—that is, "who they are and their level of passion for CIT," according to a sheriff's office CIT coordinator. Thus, the job of marketing to stakeholders and the community is never-ending. Such diligence avoids complacency on the part of those being served as well as unrealistic expectations.

Effective Practice

Continuously redefine program scope as the gap between capacity and demand becomes apparent.

During operations, you'll have to guard against the opposing emotions of complacency and exuberance. Once classes are regularly scheduled and CIT officers are handling calls, the tendency for program personnel is to hail victory and move to the next municipal crisis to solve. However, this is the time to redouble efforts to smooth operations in preparation for permanency and possible expansion.

Those who see the potential of CIT may want to immediately jump to changing their agency or municipality on a wide scale and consequently overreach. Guard against both by simply being realistic. This comes from a thorough understanding of your program capacity to deliver services and how much can be done well.

All stakeholders and trainees know the target population and their jurisdictional characteristics. Resources, mainly trained officers, service specific areas guided by the need to deliver a quality CIT response, arresting only as a last resort. Dispatch a CIT certified officer judiciously until capacity can match need. You want to avoid spreading officers too thin or taxing them with inappropriate calls. The CIT advisory body should be ready for a spike in calls for service from consumers and families once consumers realize they will be treated respectfully and be referred to appropriate services. This is another reason to start small. Revisit scope on a regular basis.

Automating Evaluation and Analysis for Continuous Feedback

To answer the dual needs of efficiency (enhancing process efficiencies) and effectiveness (measuring and understanding impact), you'll need to continuously evaluate and analyze the program. Use the notes that call takers/ dispatchers, responding officers, and crisis response team members take to adjust the flow of channeling consumers properly.

Effective Practice

Automate process monitoring (efficiency) and impact analysis (effectiveness) as much as possible.

Take stock of the numbers that are meaningful. Monitor especially the (criminal justice) savings of diversion to facilitate real-time data entry by staff at decision points, such as at a magistrate's office or through the jail CIT coordinator. Yes, people will still have to input data to computerize your information for evaluation and analysis. However, once you have an updatable digital picture of processes and results, it will enhance your operations exponentially. Most agencies are blessed with automation professionals. Make sure during the planning phase that they understand your automation needs for arranging data to improve operations and analysis. The best systems can be updated in real time by those closest to the data point. For example, the CIT coordinator, the executive director, and perhaps the CIT training coordinator will likely be entering data. Make sure it all comes together in a cogent, summative statement of how and how well you are doing.

Automation doesn't have to be complex; available laptops and off-the-shelf software such as Excel are enough. Automation can be something as simple as filling out a common, simple form or spreadsheet (recommended) to tally what's important to your CIT stakeholders, especially your criminal justice constituents, and the mission of diversion. For example, monitor the:

- *rates of injuries,*
- *time spent maintaining custody,*
- *time it takes the crisis response team to assume responsibility* for the consumer, and
- *number of diversions* from each decision point, starting from the call, to the responding officer, to the magistrate, to the jail, and perhaps to a mental health court.

Good ideas come from the CIT coordinator, for example, who may debrief a responding officer fresh from a CIT call. A word of caution on obtaining debriefings: Make sure you have a sworn officer do the debriefing because a question of legality may arise.

Always question how processes can be improved. After experience determines the baseline numbers, establish targets for improvement. Be prepared for criticisms or questions, the most strident of which are, "What determines a diversion?" and "Who decides when a diversion has occurred?" The answer is simple: When the call for service results in an alternative to arrest, it's considered (and counted as) a diversion.

Remember this tally is meaningful only if it's used, and its best use, again, is to compute costs savings with diversion. You'll realize savings way beyond the costs of your CIT program. Be as accurate as you can, or at least conservative, if you have to estimate numbers and what they mean; the impact to the system will still be dramatic. It's wise not to overpromise and underdeliver. Anticipate being challenged on your numbers. Celebrate and publicize successes. Always send out the results three ways—far, wide, and often. By this, you create the all-important goodwill and support for the day when—not if—you need both.

Developing Resources: Marketing Tools to Funding Streams

Maintaining essential contacts is simple but not easy. It's easier to get caught up in the busyness of training people and responding to calls. Developing support involves constantly promoting CIT at any and all meetings, agencies, and occasions that will accommodate the CIT message.

Effective Practice

Develop and use an array of marketing tools to get the word out.

Naturally, all stakeholders have a part in delivering the message. Integrated Family Services of North Carolina has a product that serves as a mailer, information stand brochure, or talking points for a presentation. (See Appendix: CIT Mobile Crisis Management Fact Sheet.) Once the message is committed to print, anyone can deliver it.

Extend the fact sheet idea further by reducing the information to a card of essential emergency contact information, which can conveniently be tucked into the visor of a (patrol) car.

Still, the best advertisement for CIT will be the growing number of successful responses to calls for service.

Choosing Preferred Trainees

The discussion of developing CIT training cannot be complete without mentioning an important characteristic of the preferred trainee. The best students are those who want to work with the mental health consumer.[77]

Effective Practice

Choose law enforcement trainees who want to work with mental health consumers.

As one study observes, "An officer with experience responding to situations involving people with mental illness in crisis or working with community resources will often have a good understanding of the issues involved."[78] Students with the best chance of success on a CIT call for service will more than likely have good communication skills, especially in active listening and perceptive interviewing. They will be patient and calm and able to gradually control a situation rather than take command quickly, which may be more appropriate for non-CIT situations.[79]

Expect well-run classes to be in constant revision. The environment of the consumer and community is in constant flux, which should be reflected in course offerings. Remain alert to maintaining a full slate of quality instructors.

> Remember to equip graduating officers with a current list of community resources. The Wake County, North Carolina, 40-hour CIT training provides each graduate with a laminated sheet of current services, agencies, and professionals for consumer referrals. This sheet is not only a practical ready reference, it's an essential tool for the consumer call.

Next, let's consider the key staff of your program.

Key Staff and the First Responder, the Essential Diversion Team

Key staff revolve around the training. The main responsibility for maintaining continued interest in a class and from class to class lies with the instructors. Although a law enforcement officer oversees each class, most of the classes are taught by trained mental health specialists, who must be able to connect with sworn officers. Still, a few of the classes are facilitated or taught by trained law enforcement professionals, which is preferable if one can be enticed to teach. They've been "in the trenches" and understand the situation on a gut level.

The mental health discipline and law enforcement require different personality traits in their practitioners. Officers may view the mental health specialist as one who doesn't understand the necessary laws, regulations, and, at times, danger that goes with their job. Plus, they may think people in the social services are "soft on crime." Mental health practitioners may hold a stereotypical view of the "cuff 'em and stuff 'em" cop that's far from the truth. These opinions must be alleviated, and the opposing factions need to agree by realizing the value of both factions to CIT.

Cooperation starts with the CIT coordinator, who chooses and prepares instructors for this mutual environment. Agreement is facilitated by the law enforcement officer in charge of the class, who sets the stage for interaction with therapists and providers.

Effective Practice

Maintain a core group of mental health services instructors who identify and connect with first responders.

Securing a Core Group of Mental Health Instructors

Instructors who succeed in communicating the message of the consumer's world are those who can keep trainees engaged. Perhaps they make the class fun by telling relevant stories or facilitate lively discussions of the point at hand. Certainly, they engage students with role playing and the intense give and take that comes from a good consumer panel. Such panels help the officers see a person with mental health issues as someone who, for the most part, has a productive life.

Good instructors learn from their students, paying close attention to class critiques and adjusting presentations accordingly. They must be in tune with the class of the moment, as each class is different. One CIT coordinator commented that her successful instructors learn to "laugh at themselves a bit." They also keep the class exciting by relating to the audience in their terms. Good instructors know their students are there because they want to make a difference by being police officers. In the case of CIT students, they know they can help consumers. Consequently, they want to learn how the regulated world of the law can fit with the chaotic world of the consumer. In this respect, the CIT coordinator continues to be pivotal.

Effective Practice

Have the CIT coordinator be responsible to the lead law enforcement executive.

Clarifying a CIT Coordinator's Role

Eastern (North) Carolina Behavioral Health has a CIT coordinator in the dual roles of working at the LME while also interfacing with the sheriff, an ardent supporter of CIT. She's the sheriff's CIT liaison. She collects data for him from the LME and from officers, sets up classes with the sheriff's approval, and provides publicity. She's detail oriented and organized, maintaining fresh classroom materials and keeping CIT in the public eye. She can substitute for an instructor who cancels at the last minute and is aware of community issues and resources. Naturally, she's passionately dedicated to the concept of CIT and believes in a consumer's self-sufficiency. She remains the CIT champion of many champions.

This CIT coordinator constructs classes as a law enforcement experience—not as lectures by social workers. She gets it. Her duties are much, much more than most coordinator duties because she serves a large catchment area. However, the main characteristic of her progress with CIT is that she has a clear responsibility to the sheriff for the success of it. This relationship strengthens the results of CIT. At the very least, regular and frequent diversions occur during calls and from the sheriff's jail.

Good instructors learn from their students, paying close attention to class critiques and adjusting presentations accordingly. They must be in tune with the class of the moment, as each class is different.

The well-run program has a most accommodating relationship with the local community college (at least in North Carolina), where classes are regularly conducted. The CIT coordinator makes that connection. A local two-year technical college is the perfect place for CIT training because it's set up for the educational experience. The community college accurately tracks curriculum changes, thoroughly gleans good ideas from evaluations, and collects CIT data sheets on an ongoing basis. Plus, coffee is always nearby.

The CIT coordinator also ensures that marketing messages spread to the wider community via a range of printed materials, presentations, and workshops.

A sheriff's CIT coordinator commented she knew CIT had "arrived" when a mental health consumer and family asked for a CIT officer when they were in crisis.

The example of a well-run program means more law enforcement agencies want the model. One CIT coordinator sponsors "lunch and learn" sessions for any group that wants to hear how CIT works. She also administers a local website.

A sheriff's CIT coordinator commented that she knew CIT had "arrived" when a mental health consumer and family asked for a CIT officer when they were in crisis. More and more stories of successes flood in—and more officers volunteer to be CIT officers. The community embraces CIT. Even in some of the most austere times and in rural settings, this reform movement progresses toward Capacity Building, matrix solutions to local social ills, and values/character-driven leadership and team building.

One of the original champions of CIT in North Carolina captured what CIT means for the community. She said it represents the rare local service that sets out to make a difference in a problem and does just that. It's the next generation of governance composed of a matrix of people and agencies collaborating for a common cause built on trust. Trust is the key, says a leading NAMI advocate—trust that the officer, LME staff, and community-based service providers will do their best to keep the consumer in the community and as productive as his or her abilities will allow.

CIT, when done by Capacity Building, is self-perpetuating, flexible, and dynamic, while providing the structure for continuous growth. It has the capacity to make a significant difference in community livability and be socially transformative.

"Security is not the meaning of my life.
Great opportunities are worth the risk."
– Shirley Hufstedler

Chapter 5

PHASE III. SUSTAIN AND EXPAND

Chapter 5

PHASE III. SUSTAIN AND EXPAND

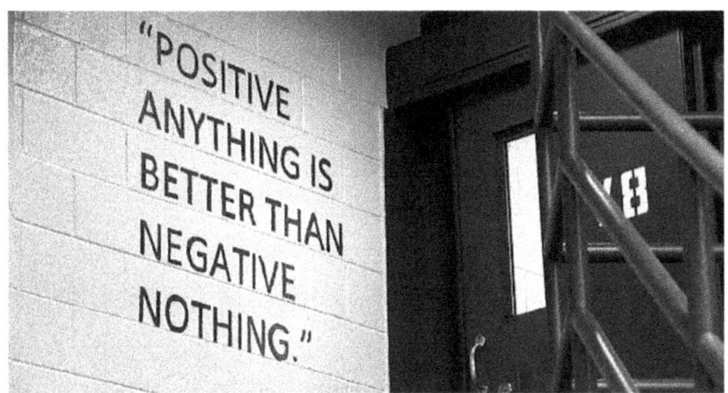

Encouraging Quote on the Wall Inside the Yavapai County, Arizona, Jail's Mental Health Unit

"New and stirring things are belittled because if they are not belittled, the humiliating question arises, 'Why then are you not taking part in them?'"
– H. G. Wells

Your CIT program should now be relatively routine. Classes are regularly scheduled; the ranks of qualified CIT first responders are growing. The word about CIT is spreading throughout and beyond the community, and you have the confidence of repeated successful problem resolutions. You're well beyond the potentially crippling problems of inadequate planning and implementation.

Your advisory board has made the successful transition from planning to program oversight. They've anticipated the day when the program can grow to close the gap between needs and services. CIT coordinators at law enforcement agencies and the LME have a working collaboration. Select community resources are fully engaged in providing services for CIT referrals. The plan for stability is based on building capacity for services delivery and relationships with key stakeholders.

The scope of responsibilities expands as resources and supporting capacity materialize. The team is collecting, analyzing, and disseminating simple data, especially concerning the impact of diversions. Suggestions from people handling and responding to calls are continually smoothing out processes.

The core of instructors is in sync with the needs of law enforcement in general and the student body in particular. The LME CIT coordinator has a great working relationship with law enforcement executives, especially police chiefs and the sheriff. Program practitioners are delivering CIT services to create lasting and positive changes in community safety, security, and well-being. In other words—CIT is a community fixture.

Taking CIT Forward

Now you can begin to further assess/question your service-to-needs gap. Use the reliable data you've accumulated from calls and their results. You might ask: How many suicides were prevented? What are the caseloads for affected clinicians? How many consumers are waiting for a place in day treatment? By the time you're ready to expand, you'll have a clear idea of CIT first responders' workloads. Do their rates of diversion, time saved in transferring custody, or the number of calls for service and general CIT duties justify a full-time CIT position in the sheriff's office?

According to a lead police executive, CIT has arrived when:

- diversion is seen as the norm,
- mental illness is recognized as a treatable disability,
- services are available for the people living with mental illness, and
- CIT is seen as a viable tool for law enforcement because it's not only smart *about* crime but tough on crime.

Change and improvement is welcomed; expansion is not only possible but also inevitable if considered a goal of the program. You've been working toward the cusp of scaling your program. You can now begin to expand to close the services-to-needs gap—an enviable state of affairs for any public service.

Sustaining Operations by Continuous Redefinition

At this stage of program Capacity Building, decriminalizing the mentally ill in your community is not only commonplace but also expected. It's time to revisit how much the program can accomplish and still do things well. Experience cautions not to "let the horse out of the barn before the fence is up." Before you expand a jurisdiction or address a different population (e.g., schools) or anticipate 24/7 CIT response, ensure the capacity of crisis response and drop-off capability are in place. Also make sure MOUs guide your procedures, protocols match expectations, and everything is legal.

Effective Practice

Redefine scope: Restate vision, mission, and goals.

As you redefine, the vision of decriminalizing the people living with mental illness will probably remain the same. You can modify the mission, however, to improve crisis response. This may be possible with a permanent crisis response center devoted to a single county with the resources to support it. Or perhaps a larger catchment area of several counties can fund one crisis assessment center by pooling resources.

A good mission would be to expand from diversion at a call for service to diversion at any decision point before incarceration. This means diverting a consumer from jail by a social worker, by the magistrate, or by a judge, for example. The CIT mentality considers any diversion from jail a diversion, no matter where or when it happens.

Another goal could be to increase the percentage of sworn officers trained or oriented to CIT by agency or by region. You might adapt training to wider circles of first responders, including fire fighters, EMTs, or school resource officers, for example. School resource officers will need specialized training in handling teen mental health needs, especially suicide prevention. Assess whether your training is adequate for all first responders, jail personnel, and telecommunicators. As one officer points out, "You really don't know what (skills) you're missing until you need them." The message is that CIT training needs to continually evolve and the community can benefit from officers who are continually updated with better/more current techniques of diversion. One of the original CIT core partners suggests the following.

- At the *local* level:
    - *Keep communication open* – Tailor training to assessed demands. Expedite the preparation and update of informational data sheets and keep information flowing to all who need to know.
    - *Systematize agency CIT liaisons* – Make each (law enforcement) agency self-sufficient in CIT by assigning a CIT coordinator to each agency.
    - *Assess the service-to-needs gap* – Keep data points meaningful to funders. By computing the costs of an arrest and possible incarceration and comparing it to the savings of the CIT diversion effort, you can show increasing savings and justify continued/increasing resources support. For example:
        - *Admissions* – Monitor admissions to emergency rooms, which is a measure of how an emergency drop-off is working. A decrease in the frequency of admissions indicates the efficiency and effectiveness of CIT beat officers.
        - *Time invested* – Monitor how much time an officer spends in an emergency room with a consumer. This time indicates the success, or lack thereof, of the emergency drop-off function. A reduction in time spent translates to costs saved. Keep good records, as some may argue a difference in time spent.
- At the *regional* level – Consider the unique needs of a region. For example, there may be a region-wide concern for teen mental health, which can be addressed with specialized training for school resource officers or a teen court to keep juveniles from the criminal justice system. In outreach to youth, proactively post CIT information in the schools and engage administrators and parent/teacher organizations to build goodwill and credibility. Following a disastrous event, even in a neighboring county or across the country, there may be students or others who emotionally fall apart or act out. CIT is a great resource.
- At the *state* level – Perhaps it's time for a statewide CIT association to share information more widely, brainstorm systemic concerns, and maintain

uniformity of services delivery and standards of operation. Develop statewide data—always a concern and critical to telling the CIT story.

Focus on understanding and improving processes. The purpose of this is to avoid the petition (to commit) or arrest in the first place. Focus on a target population. Notice the continuing theme, *especially* during expansion, of doing less but doing it well, not doing more. Whatever the level of focus, have a rollout plan sanctioned by law enforcement. Match trainees with class content and make sure they can be released to that class for the full length of the training. A transition team of the key stakeholders and law enforcement leadership would prove valuable. Be inclusive—up to a practical point. Perhaps the state sheriffs' and police chiefs' associations can endorse the expansion plan.

Prepare for Detractors

Don't expect 100 percent participation. While praiseworthy partnerships are ideal, establishing them is not universal. Some groups or individuals will never fully understand what CIT does. Those committed to CIT are stretched quite thin: One sheriff's deputy has full duties as a sergeant and runs the countywide CIT operations for the sheriff. Be prepared for obstructionism.

"Noise proves nothing—often a hen who has merely laid an egg cackles as if she had laid an asteroid."
- Mark Twain

One of the first criticisms aired is usually about lack of cooperation between law enforcement and social service agencies. Only a steady stream of true successes of cooperation and collaboration can answer this uninformed continuous refrain.

Whatever the level of focus, have a rollout plan sanctioned by law enforcement. Match trainees with class content and make sure they can be released to that class for the full length of the training.

Next, detractors will say the community has "no mental health services." How then, the objection continues, can there be a true diversion when the consumer goes untreated? A crisis services director observes he simply can't completely serve the neediest of consumers. However, even with an extreme lack of services, alternatives to incarceration often exist, and those must be stressed. Pursue these alternatives during planning and implementation so they may be used during the development of the program. Many diversions happen when an officer has a services referral brochure for ready reference. And don't forget that families stand ready to intervene and divert.

Considering the lack of services, another argument states, "We are asking too much of CIT." The answer to that is to balance demand and capability. Some consumers will continue to struggle to get the right or adequate services; that's inevitable. Serve those you can, the best you can. The greatest hope for more services is long-term work on the continuum of care. That's why the immediate focus is on diversion to the best possible alternative to jail.

Other detractors will say, "CIT has no basis in science," thereby dismissing CIT as having no evidence of success. Ah, the refrain of the obstructionist who has run out of objections and still wants to pester the willing and the doers. That argument turns a blind eye to the impressive numbers of diversions. True, the evidence of data remains a big problem. That's why this model stresses monitoring a few measures meaningful to decision makers—especially in law enforcement. Hence, the importance of the dollar savings to jails and the time saved for police work by first responders.

Some argue CIT will result in more drop-offs (at an emergency department or a crisis assessment center) than there's capability to accommodate. If so, this is a discrepancy in capacity, which will need to be documented and addressed.

Many diversions happen when an officer has a services referral brochure for ready reference.

Last, one argument states, "Someone has to pick up the expenses of treating the mental health consumer, and CIT is only transferring those expenses to other public services." True in a sense. However, expenses are being transferred from jails to community and state services and agencies that are much better equipped than jails to treat consumers. Incarceration is the least efficient and effective and most expensive alternative. Save the cell for those who really need it.

"Knee jerk" reactions to a call for mental services suggest crisis response is being presented as *the* answer to the problem of a consumer in crisis. Rather, the focus needs to be on the available services and how to access them. Far more debilitating results arise from unnecessarily incarcerating a consumer, especially for a misdemeanor, than from relying on "less-than-ideal" community alternatives to arrest.

Ultimately, if the drumbeat of opposition is overpowering, perhaps it's not the best time to expand, or perhaps the plans for expansion can be scaled back. However, be patient, keep records, continue the good work, and spread the word. CIT's time to expand will come.

Plotting Your Long-Range Strategy and Tactics for Scaling Up

Look at a comprehensive strategy for jail diversion. Encompass pre- and post-booking. Consider mental health courts, jail diversion, and community-based corrections that focus on integrating the consumer into the community, away from the criminal justice system. With this focus, the CIT program becomes part of a reentry strategy that encompasses keeping children in primary and secondary school as well as juvenile and adult reentry.

A successful LME director maintaining a 24/7 crisis assessment center shared advice for securing resources for the long-range strategy of having CIT become a permanent presence:

- *Stay committed* – CIT is at a crucial nascent point in its development as an accepted strategy. Naysayers could drown out any progress. Continue monthly and, at least, quarterly meetings.
- *Persist* – Connect to the community. Talk about money, how much is needed, where to get it, and where it will do the most good. This director vowed she wouldn't retire until CIT was institutionalized statewide. That's the necessary attitude when a good idea struggles to become part of the community fabric.
- *Share the work, vision, mission, and goals* – Development needs to be a communal effort. Construct the networked matrix of CIT service providers. Share resources. Share space. Publicize good CIT works and needs. Keep up the drumbeat of cost-effectiveness.
- *Renew MOUs* – It's most helpful to reenergize leadership with an annual renewal of agreements. Strive for uniformity in MOUs and consistency in the services offered at the various training sites. Share ideas for how crisis response teams can work better and thoughts on how to replicate the CIT approach according to the process of Capacity Building.

Remember, the goal is to create spaces, environments, and ways for as many people as possible to have the chance to realistically thrive to the best of their abilities.

- *Work for community services* – Never let up on expanding community services—public, private, and private nonprofit. Consumers need the means to conduct their lives, including housing, reliable/regular transportation, a trade and meaningful job, support systems, and treatment. Remember, the goal is to create spaces, environments, and ways for as many people as possible to have the chance to realistically thrive to the best of their abilities.
- *Take failure in stride* – Interest may wane. A crisis assessment center may diminish due to lack of funding. Keep the idea alive with the core of first responders who know CIT works.

Effective Practice

Continue to strengthen the comprehensive jail diversion network.

Remember that diversion can happen with the magistrates and with pre-trial re-entry counselors, who can put a consumer on pre-trial supervision. Charges can be dismissed, or the consumer can be put on pre-trial release during the first appearance at court.

Much has been said throughout this model about diversion from jail. Perhaps now, during the expansion of your CIT effort, you can hire a full-time jail CIT co-ordinator. Ask local court officials if it's time to begin a mental health court.

Remember the cardinal rule of scope: Expand based only on the capacity to do so. The municipality can survive via a transition team. Perhaps build a pilot site: Call it a "CIT Center of Excellence," for example, where jail diversion is done as well as possible to demonstrate what should and especially can be done

---

Effective Practice

Assemble a transition team to close the services-to-needs gap.

Expansion to Rural Areas

Probably the trickiest issue, yet with the greatest potential for CIT, is its expansion to rural areas. The small-town police chief with a handful of sworn officers or the sheriff in a remote county face unique difficulty. Mainly, they have even more austere fiscal conditions as well as inadequate personnel, both of which are stretched to remarkable limits. How, for example, can a sheriff's deputy attend training when he or she may be one of only a few officers on a shift? Therefore, a law enforcement official in a remote area might investigate how much money could be saved by jail diversion. Then, he or she can make the case that CIT doesn't cost, it pays; because the money saved can easily pay for a CIT coordinator and attendant CIT expenses.

Remember the cardinal rule of scope: Expand based only on the capacity to do so.

Wisdom from CIT Successes

As with all good ideas, everything CIT touches improves; the collateral, unintended benefits are pleasantly surprising. The community coalesces around a common problem and together makes a real difference while becoming an example for how cooperation and especially collaboration with a silo-busting matrix of services and people can work.

CIT is 21st-century governance at its finest. It brings out the best in people. The idea of CIT continues to have a striking effect on participating agencies, individual workers, and especially mental health clients and their families. CIT supports the principles of Capacity Building in that it encourages everyone participating to be the best they can be, to stretch and grow, and to collaborate for the greater good.

CIT transforms many stereotypes, ideas, ways of doing business, and expectations. Following are discoveries this program has brought to light:

- *Officers don't want to arrest a consumer.* The law enforcement officer of today is not the stereotypical Hollywood bad actor with a badge and an edge. Officers of today epitomize leading with intellect and compassion and sincerely want to make a difference in their communities. When involved in CIT, they work to make a positive difference in the lives of mental health consumers.

- *It's surprising how much can be done with so little.* People can always find just a little more energy to do one more thing. CIT will work just about anywhere people have the will to face down obstacles and persist with the

CIT is 21st-century governance at its finest. It brings out the best in people.

idea—even if it takes years to make this new way of delivering public services from the bottom up accepted and permanent.

- *Everyone wins with CIT—especially the consumer.* CIT creates believers. Everyone interviewed was fully aware of the frustrations of starting up and running a program. Yet they remained remarkably enthused and very willing to take the next step or lend a hand. Despite lack of funding, obstructionism, and inertia, even the "old hands," who could well have been worn down, looked forward to doing more.
- *A single-agency answer to community problems isn't the way to go.* The matrix agency solution works. This CIT model demonstrates how resources can be combined to answer social dysfunction and service needs. It's all about the process. When one of these network solutions to a local problem such as CIT is started, the process can be applied to many other concerns.
- *A process based on Capacity Building works.* Focusing on the capacity to resolve a problem rather than just delivering a service takes the focus off people and the inevitable behavioral dynamics and puts it on the practicalities of solving the problem.
- *People want reform.* Although people can have great energy around changing the way things are, they can be confused about how to do it. Inertia and complacency set in. CIT brings out the compassion of neighbors helping neighbors and the desire to make things better for one another. It helps them become more aware of community. Solutions to bureaucracy and stereotyping happen with CIT. The program demonstrates that structural and human impediments to progress can be ameliorated with a matrix of local services designed to decriminalize the mental ill.
- *Crisis response is vital and can be made to work.* Crucial to the success of CIT is crisis response by mental health providers who can accept custody of the consumer.
- *Law enforcement and providers must cooperate* for the sake of the consumer, which minimizes turf disputes.
- *Vision, mission, and goals must be fluid, dynamic, and organic.* Decriminalizing people living with mental illness is a moving target. It's made more complex by the necessity to tailor the basic idea to each locality that tries it.

Yes, the overall goal of decriminalizing the mental health consumer remains the driving force. But the goals to get there reflect local dynamics and the complexity of helping the target population. The situation is different in a small rural jurisdiction with quite limited resources from that of a large metropolitan area. What's done and how it's done constantly evolve.

- *Data is paramount.* When planning, settle the issue of what information will be collected, how it will be analyzed, and especially how it will be disseminated. Do this with the understanding of who needs to know about CIT and what interests them.
- *Diversion is first about saving money.* No matter how compelling the moral justification is for decriminalizing consumers, the case for saving money is the *first* reason people buy into CIT and continue their interest. Deciding to do anything in the public sector is not a matter of simply choosing something and doing it; it's a difficult matter of choosing this at the expense of that.
- *CIT operations aim for permanency.* It's easy for operations to devolve into dealing only with looming crises, whether they're with consumers or the falling out of participants. Focusing on Capacity Building in pursuit of permanency will direct your limited resources—especially time—toward the primary program goal of becoming self-sustaining. Capacity Building is process oriented not project oriented, which takes much of the negative personal dynamics out of the work.
- *Permanency spreads the benefits of CIT to the wider community.* A well running, self-sufficient CIT program will result in measurable decreases in consumer arrests, re-arrests, commitments, and incarcerations, at the very least. This, in turn, makes the community safer and more secure, on the way to becoming a place in which to thrive.
- *Mental disease can be treated.* CIT teaches that mental health is a physical condition that can be resolved, not a problem for our institutions to cure. Much can be done simply by the consumer and family accepting responsibility for positive outcomes. This acceptance is augmented by consumer-aware institutional and professional assistance.

- *We can reduce the number of mental health consumers in jail.* Jails will always be burdened. CIT programming is a significant way to relieve some of this persistent, pervasive problem. It's difficult to "see" the decline in incarcerated populations with diversion. But indeed, CIT reduces the need for criminal justice responses to mental illness while reserving precious public resources for those who need it more urgently.

Life after arrest was exceedingly tough for the consumer before CIT, according to a lead NAMI official. After arrest, the patient was thrust into a different life. He or she probably got a record and became a problem to society, with little chance for dignity and capability.

With CIT, the consumer gains a sense of self-esteem and a place in the community. The participating agency now has a new role to play in achieving social transformation.

CIT is an important and proven solution to the problems caused by closing mental hospitals and curtailing public services for the people living with mental illness. It's an answer to jail over-crowding and an effective reentry aftercare for people who cycle in and out of the criminal justice system. It's a proven model for how to address local public service issues and a process that is replicable. CIT must be introduced to as many communities as possible.

The CIT Capacity Building Tool for Diversion Success

Please note and use the CIT Capacity Building Checklist with Key Action Items and Effective Practices given both on pages 2 to 4 and pages 153 to 155 in the Appendix. It encapsulates the process you've read about in this book. Use it as a general guide. It suggests a necessary order and priority of activities that keep the work focused on essential tasks.

Will you follow this checklist to the letter? Hardly! Will you enhance your chance of success by adopting a unique process based on building capacity? Oh yes!

The best way to start is to review this life cycle guide of essential Capacity Building and consider each associated action item. You'll have a viable tool to decriminalize people living with mental illness and continuously improve the well-being of your community.

Consider accepting the invitation to become virtue- and character-driven. By building your CIT capacity for permanency from the bottom up with matrices of local talent and resources, with persistence and determination—you will succeed. With that, you win, your colleagues win, your agency wins, and your community wins—as never before. By your personal growth and the success of your CIT program, you'll provide an example of character-based leadership with implications far into the future and way beyond your career.

Thank you for your service!

ABOUT THE AUTHORS

JAMES KLOPOVIC, Major, USAF, retired, holds a Doctor of Public Policy (DPP) from Charles Sturt University, Sydney, Australia, with concentration on service program capacity building at the organizational and community levels.

James is helping cultivate the next generation of leaders via character-based education and development. He promotes the understanding of how to build teams that accomplish more than the sum of the parts and combines this passion with developing better ways to deliver municipal public services with collaborative Capacity Building.

After retiring from the United States Air Force, James continued providing leadership at federal, state, and local levels for a total of 45 years. He served as a senior staffer for 25 years on the North Carolina Governor's Crime Commission, where his responsibilities encompassed strategic planning, municipal governance, financial development, federal granting, and community and organizational development, implementation, and evaluation. Now he writes, publishes, and consults.

One of the numerous programs he created detailed the processes and procedures for School Resource Officers, which resulted in continuously improving learning environments statewide while making schools safer. Those programs continue today.

As the principal investigator/program director on a series of research programs, he analyzed and proposed model local programs leading to grant proposals for dozens of municipal and state initiatives. He has broad experience in logistics, training, and education. His expertise in program design, implementation, and management includes ensuring program and organizational permanency. His technical support to numerous local government entities created and enhanced service ideas such as delinquency prevention, reentry, and decriminalizing people living with mental illness.

James is cofounder of The Nicole and James Klopovic Family Charitable Foundation, which lends support to local social programs with funding and knowledge of Capacity Building to encourage *Permanent Solutions to Permanent Problems.*

He has authored numerous publications regarding community policing, community development, and effective/efficient delivery of public services as well as books for fun. In descending order of date, they include the following:

The Good Life: My Legacy for You. A memoir. (Morrisville, N.C.: Affinitas Publishing, 2023) Available through Amazon and *http://www.affinitaspublishing.org.*

Volume I, Capacity Building Series: *Building Capacity from the Bottom Up: The Key to Sustaining Local Services.* (Morrisville, N.C.: Affinitas Publishing, 2024) Available through Amazon and *http://www.affinitaspublishing.org.*

Volume II, Capacity Building Series: *Decriminalizing Mental Illness: A Practical Guide for Building Sustainable Crisis Intervention Teams.* (Morrisville, N.C.: Affinitas Publishing, Second Edition 2024) Available through Amazon and *http://www.affinitaspublishing.org.*

Volume III, Capacity Building Series: *Accelerating Juvenile Reentry: A Practical Capacity Building Model for Sustaining Aftercare.* (Morrisville, N.C.: Affinitas Publishing, 2024) Available through Amazon and *http://www.affinitaspublishing.org.*

Volume IV, Capacity Building Series: *Accelerating Adult Reentry: A Practical Capacity Building Model for Sustaining Post-Release Transitional Services.* (Morrisville, N.C.: Affinitas Publishing, 2024) Available through Amazon and *http://www.affinitaspublishing.org.*

Becoming a New Wave Leader: Principles and Practices to Live and Lead Well. (Morrisville, N.C.: Affinitas Publishing, 2021) Available through Amazon and *http://www.affinitaspublishing.org.*

Your Moral Compass: A Practical Guide for New Wave Leaders. (2020) Available through Amazon and *http://www.affinitaspublishing.org.*

Little Stories: A Legacy of Living, Laughing and Loving. (Morrisville, N.C.: Affinitas Publishing, 2019) Available through Amazon and *http://www.affinitaspublishing.org.*

The Honest Backpacker: A Practical Guide for the Rookie Adventurer over 50. (Morrisville, N.C.: Affinitas Publishing, 2017) Available through Amazon and *http://www.affinitaspublishing.org.*

Effective Program Practices for At-Risk Youth: A Continuum of Community Based Programs. (Kingston, N.J.: Civic Research Institute, Inc., 2003). Available through Amazon and *https://civicresearchinstitute.com/index.html.*

Contact: *jklopovic@gmail.com*

NICOLE KLOPOVIC is the daughter of James Klopovic. She holds a Doctor of Medical Science and is a certified Physician Associate (PA-C), practicing in the areas of Emergency Medicine, Urgent Care, Aesthetics, Weight Management, and Primary Care. In addition, she is a captain in the U.S. Air Force Reserve Medical Corps and is pursuing her Air Force career concurrently with her career as a PA-C.

She stays active with dance instructing, weightlifting, hiking, and cycling and enjoys cooking and traveling, striving to embrace the motto *carpe diem* while maintaining her passion to mentor, help, and teach others.

Nicole is cofounder and CEO of The Nicole and James Klopovic Family Charitable Foundation, which lends support to local social programs with funding and knowledge of Capacity Building to encourage *Permanent Solutions to Permanent Problems.*

APPENDIX

CIT Capacity Building Checklist

This checklist (also shown upfront in How to Get the Most Out of this Book on pages 2 to 4) is only a point of departure. You'll need to modify it—and in fact, any checklist—to suit your unique set of circumstances.

You'll never have perfect and full information, and it isn't necessary. What matters is that you act. Reality will teach you the path to realize an efficient, effective, and (especially) self-sustaining CIT program.

This overall checklist will help the matrix team of planners eventually arrive at the collective realization that "Today is the day we quit planning and do it." It is followed by other checklists, procedures, and plans to give you a comprehensive head start and guides for the various aspects of your program.

Fig. 1-B. CIT Capacity Building Checklist – PHASES I-III, with Key Action Items and Effective Practices
PHASE I of the Project Life Cycle: Plan and Implement
1. Nurture and grow key leadership. Assemble your core group of CIT champions and leaders.
Assemble a core group of change agents responsible for making CIT happen.
State your CIT vision, mission, goals, and values as guides to daily decision making.
Assemble key stakeholders and get buy-in.
Meet regularly in an organized fashion with an emphasis on purpose.
Organize work by functional committees and standardized operations.
2. Develop a strategic plan.
Develop an action-oriented strategic plan.
3. Determine project scope.
Develop project scope by mapping clientele and community resources.
Assess readiness to implement CIT.
Establish a 24/7, no-refusal crisis response.

4.	**Map local services and create a common playbook.**
	Map local services that are alternatives to arrest for law enforcement.
5.	**Design impact analysis.**
	Understand the costs of arrest to develop an argument for CIT.
	Develop essential measurements of decriminalizing individuals with mental illness that appeal to key stakeholders.
6.	**Nurture relationships.**
	Develop relationships to secure resources beyond money.
	Develop marketing strategies
7.	**Develop training to fit both officers and consumers.**
	Design CIT training to fit both law enforcement and the mental health consumer.
8.	**Develop staff for performance and team effort.**
	Choose law enforcement-oriented CIT coordinators.
	Choose performance-oriented CIT class instructors.
	PHASE II: Operate and Stabilize
9.	**Plan operations with the future in mind. Gear leadership for permanency.**
	Establish a CIT advisory board for oversight and necessary work.
	Strengthen the CIT collaborative between law enforcement and mental health CIT coordinators.
	Pilot your first 40-hour CIT class with officers from one sheriff's office.
	Continuously build and rebuild your community-based resources.
	Actively pursue your plan for CIT stability.
	Continuously redefine program scope as the gap between capacity and demand becomes apparent.
	Automate process monitoring (efficiency) and impact analysis (effectiveness) as much as possible.
	Develop and use an array of marketing tools to get the word out.
	Choose law enforcement trainees who want to work with mental health consumers.

Maintain a core group of mental health services instructors who identify and connect with first responders.
Have the CIT coordinator be responsible to the lead law enforcement executive.
PHASE III: Sustain and Expand
10. Sustain operations by continuous redefinition.
Redefine scope: Restate vision, mission, and goals.
11. Plot your long-range strategy and tactics for scaling up.
Continue to strengthen the comprehensive jail diversion network.
Assemble a transition team to close the services-to-needs gap.

CIT Program Readiness Checklist

1. **Police Departments and Sheriff's Offices:**

- ❑ Ensure police officers and deputies attend four hours of observation.
- ❑ Ensure police officers and deputies attend the 40-hour classroom training.
- ❑ Ensure continuity of the Capacity Building CIT model is maintained.
- ❑ Provide CIT officers in the region to assist with evaluation during role-playing exercises.
- ❑ Ensure each police chief and sheriff signs and adheres to the MOU (Memorandum of Understanding).
- ❑ Designate a CIT coordinator within each agency.
- ❑ Ensure the CIT coordinator attends CIT organizational meetings and keeps a readiness checklist to accommodate all CIT training sessions, maintaining the integrity of the CIT program.

2. **The Community College Law Enforcement School Director:**

- ❑ Provides the classroom(s).
- ❑ Registers the officers and deputies.
- ❑ Provides certificates upon graduation of CIT training.
- ❑ Develops the third-party contract with the local NAMI or nonprofit organization (NPO) host.
- ❑ Attends CIT organizational meetings as needed.

3. The Local Management Entity (LME):

- ❑ Ensures a 24/7 drop-off capability—or that a uniform screening instrument is implemented to conduct a telephonic triage for consumers and families by using the required LME Screening, Triage & Referral (STR) units for Crisis Intervention Team officers.
- ❑ Identifies instructors for the CIT classroom topics.
- ❑ Provides the (four-hour) observation for officers at the ED (Emergency Department) or Crisis Center.
- ❑ Provides role players for the scenarios during the training.
- ❑ Signs the MOU.
- ❑ Designates a CIT coordinator within the agency.
- ❑ Maintains a readiness checklist to accommodate all CIT training.

4. NAMI/CFAC (Consumer and Family Advisory Committee)/Advocates' nonprofit organization:

- ❑ Act as liaisons with the Community College.
- ❑ Set up the locations for the site visits.
- ❑ Set up a consumer panel.
- ❑ Provide refreshments for the students in the classroom.
- ❑ Provide the cake-cutting ceremony at graduation.
- ❑ Sign the MOU.
- ❑ Designate a CIT coordinator in the NPO (nonprofit organization).
- ❑ Maintain a readiness checklist to accommodate all CIT training.

CIT Implementation Readiness Checklist

Note that the first section of the following readiness checklist mirrors the CIT Capacity Building Checklist. When considering readiness, it's good to be aware of the planning process you will take up in earnest when you decide you are ready to proceed. You can use this readiness checklist from the beginning of planning to check off what's complete and have an idea of tasks yet to be done.

You don't have to completely finish every action item. "Good enough" is good enough, given that an appropriate amount of thought and energy has gone into each item.

First, answer each item in the Status column. If you answer Partial or No in the Status column, roughly assess what the impact on CIT implementation might be in the Impact column. With this, you will have a visual assessment of what remains to be done and the impact of it.

Suggestions for readiness checklists are available on the internet. The format and headings in the following chart were adopted from various checklists and agencies.

CIT Pre-implementation Work Plan

Reprinted courtesy of the Virginia CIT Coalition: *https://virginiacit.org/*

ACTION STEPS	Date Assigned	Assigned To	Status/ Comments	Completed
Organizational Setup				
Establish Oversight/Steering Committee and Chairperson.				
Identify and solicit other key stakeholders not currently involved.				
Establish workgroup committees.				
Gain support of sheriff and police chiefs, if not already involved.				
Determine who will chair committees.				
Determine who will keep minutes and maintain a tracking form.				
Establish date for first 40-hour training event.				
Designate key personnel to attend CIT events in other communities.				
Implementation				
Review and revise department policies for both law enforcement and receiving facilities.				
Create an on-going system for future recruitment, registration, notification.				
Develop and hold dispatcher training.				
Develop and hold management training – 4 hours on what CIT is, what officers learn.				
Plan ongoing education opportunities, e.g., roll call.				
Plan ongoing education – e.g., posters, brochures, flyers				

ACTION STEPS	Date Assigned	Assigned To	Status/ Comments	Completed
Set up a regular meeting schedule with an oversight/ operational group that chairs and establishes frequency of meetings.				
CIT Coordinators				
Identify a CIT coordinator for each agency.				
Determine how to identify the first group of officers for training and method to register them.				
Hold general orientation for law enforcement agencies.				
Select participants for first class (determine jurisdictions).				
Notify participants of class/schedule/expectations.				
Logistics				
Secure training site, including A-Vs, nearest Crisis Center (CC) with law enforcement training.				
Secure a source of supplies/ reproduction of materials/ notebooks.				
Reproduce handouts for manual.				
Reproduce other handouts – resource cards, articles on CIT, etc.				
Determine the methods of evaluation and prepare evaluation forms.				
Order pins and diplomas (or coordinate with CC).				
Create registration and evaluation forms or coordinate with CC.				
Prepare rosters and nametags along with onsite sign-in sheets.				

ACTION STEPS	Date Assigned	Assigned To	Status/ Comments	Completed
Confirm time slots with each instructor.				
Arrange for field visits.				
Identify role players.				
Clarify who is daily training coordinator.				
Secure refreshments.				
Develop and send out press release.				
Plan for graduation – Meal? Press? Dignitaries? Guests? Speakers? Photographer?				
Hold Training Class				
Post-training Follow-up				
Process evaluations.				
Hold debriefing and review.				
Plan next 40-hour class series.				

CIT Implementation Readiness Checklist						
Item	**Status**			**Impact on CIT Implementation**		
	Yes	**Partial**	**No**	**Direct**	**Partial**	**Minimal**
I. Planning						
A. Leadership						
❑ Assemble the core group of change agents who will be responsible for making CIT happen.						
❑ Assemble key stakeholders and get buy-in.						
❑ Meet regularly in an organized fashion with an emphasis on purpose.						
❑ Organize for work by functional committee and standardized operations.						
❑ Develop an action-oriented strategic plan.						
❑ Assess readiness to implement CIT.						
B. Capacity Assessment						
❑ Establish a 24/7, no-refusal crisis response.						
❑ Map local services that are alternatives to arrest for law enforcement.						

Item	Status			Impact on CIT Implementation		
	Yes	Partial	No	Direct	Partial	Minimal
C. Project Scope						
❑ State vision, mission, goals as guides to daily decision making.						
D. Impact Analysis and Process Evaluation						
❑ Understand the costs of arrest; develop the tradeoff argument for CIT.						
❑ Develop essential measurements of decriminalizing the mentally ill that appeal to key stakeholders.						
E. Resources Development						
❑ Develop relationships to secure resources beyond money.						
F. Services						
❑ Design CIT training to fit law enforcement and the mental health consumer.						
❑ Choose law enforcement trainees who want to work with mental health consumers.						

Item	Status			Impact on CIT Implementation		
	Yes	Partial	No	Direct	Partial	Minimal
G. Key Staff						
❑ Choose law enforcement-oriented CIT coordinators.						
❑ Choose performance-oriented CIT class instructors and alternate list.						
II. Training Readiness						
A. Police Departments and the Sheriff's Office						
❑ Ensure that police officers & deputies attend 4 hrs. of observation at the hospital emergency dept. or crisis center.						
❑ Ensure officers & deputies attend the 40-hour classroom.						
❑ Ensure continuity of the Memphis model is maintained.						
❑ Provide CIT officers in the region to assist with evaluation during role plays.						
❑ Ensure police chiefs and sheriffs sign and adhere to the MOU.						
❑ Designate a CIT coordinator within each agency.						

Item	Status			Impact on CIT Implementation		
	Yes	Partial	No	Direct	Partial	Minimal
❑ Ensure the CIT coordinators attend CIT organizational meetings, maintain a readiness checklist to accommodate all CIT training sessions, and maintain the integrity of the CIT program.						
B. Community College Law Enforcement Curriculum Director						
❑ Provides the classroom(s).						
❑ Registers the officers and deputies.						
❑ Provides certificates upon graduation of CIT training.						
❑ Develops the 3rd-party contract with local NAMI or NPO host.						
❑ Attends CIT organizational meetings as needed.						
C. NAMI / CFAC / Advocates NPO						
❑ Establish liaison with the community college.						

Item	Status			Impact on CIT Implementation		
❑ Set up the locations for the site visits.						
❑ Set up a consumer panel.						
	Yes	Partial	No	Direct	Partial	Minimal
❑ Sign the Memorandum of Understanding (MOU).						
❑ Designate a CIT coordinator in the NPO organization.						
❑ Maintain a readiness checklist to accommodate all CIT training.						
❑ Provide refreshments for the students in the classroom.						
❑ Provide cake-cutting ceremony at graduation.						
D. The Local Management Entity (LME)						
❑ Ensures there's a 24/7 drop-off capability or uniform screening instrument being implemented to conduct a telephonic triage for consumers and families by using the required LME Screening, Triage & Referral (STR) units for Crisis Intervention Team officers.						

❑ Identify instructors for the CIT classroom topics.						

Item	Status			Impact on CIT Implementation		
	Yes	Partial	No	Direct	Partial	Minimal
❑ Provide the 4-hr. observation for officers at the hospital emergency department or crisis center.						
❑ Provide role players for the scenarios during the training						
❑ Sign the MOU.						
❑ Designate a CIT coordinator within the agency.						
❑ Maintain a readiness checklist to accommodate all CIT training.						

CIT 40-Hour Course Schedule Sample

	Monday (Date)	Tuesday (Date)	Wednesday (Date)	Thursday (Date)	Friday (Date)
8:00		DEVELOPMENTAL DISABILITIES (Taught by a mental health professional)	MOVIE (Select an appropriate movie.)	SITE VISIT Group A – (Select a relevant site.) Group B – (Select a relevant site.)	CRISIS INTERVENTION & DE-ESCALATION (Law enforcement instructor)
8:10	WELCOME				
8:20	REGISTRATION				
8:30	CIT OVERVIEW				
8:40					
8:50	BREAK	BREAK	BREAK		BREAK
9:00	ADVOCATES OVERVIEW (Instructed by a NAMI representative)	SUBSTANCE ABUSE (Taught by a mental health professional)	INITIATING INVOLUNTARY OR VOLUNTARY TREATMENT AT MENTAL HEALTH AND SUBSTANCE ABUSE TREATMENT FACILITIES & HIPAA (Taught by an attorney)	(Site visits facilitated by law enforcement instructors and mental health professionals)	CONNECTING TO YOUR LOCAL SERVICE NETWORKS & MOBILE CRISIS (Taught by a mental health professional)
9:10					
9:20					
9:30					
9:40					
9:50	BREAK	BREAK			BREAK
10:00	MENTAL ILLNESS AMONG CHILDREN & ADOLESCENTS (Taught by a mental health professional)	GERIATRICS & DEMENTIA (Taught by a mental health professional)		SITE VISIT (select a relevant site) (Site visits facilitated by law enforcement instructors and mental health professionals)	ROLE PLAYS (Facilitated by law enforcement instructors and mental health professionals)
10:10					
10:20					
10:30					
10:40					
10:50	BREAK	BREAK			
11:00	SYMPTOM RECOG. / ACTIVE LISTENING (Taught by a mental health professional)	PERSONALITY DISORDERS (Taught by a mental health professional)		MOVIE (Select a relevant movie.)	
11:10					
11:20					
11:30					
11:40					
11:50					

12:00 -1:00	LUNCH	LUNCH	LUNCH	LUNCH	LUNCH PROVIDED ONSITE
1:00					
1:10			TRAUMA / PTSD		
1:20		HEARING VOICES	(Taught by a mental health professional)		
1:30		(Taught by a mental health professional)			ROLE PLAYS OF CALLS FOR SERVICE BY A CONSUMER
1:40	SUICIDE				(Facilitated by law enforcement instructors and mental health professionals)
1:50			BREAK		
2:00	(Taught by a mental health professional)	MH/DD/SA & THE LOCAL ETHNIC POPULATIONS (Taught by a mental health professional)			
2:10				DE-ESCALATION SKILLS	BREAK
2:20					
2:30			MENTAL ILLNESS 101		
2:40		BREAK		(Taught by a law enforcement officer)	REVIEW
2:50	BREAK		(Taught by a mental health professional)		
3:00					
3:10					
3:20					
3:30		CONSUMER PANEL DISCUSSION			BREAK
3:40	FAMILY PANEL DISCUSSION		BREAK		
3:50					
4:00			PSYCHOTROPIC MEDICATIONS		
4:10					
4:20			(Taught by a mental health professional)		
4:30					GRADUATION
4:40		Review/Next Steps		Review/Next Steps	
4:50	Review/Next Steps				
5:00					

CIT Pre/Post-Training Questionnaire

Reprinted with permission of the School of Community and Population Health at the University of New England, Portland, Maine. *www.une.edu*

Maine CIT Expansion Project
DRAFT CIT Officer Follow-up Questionnaire

Respondent ID: __________ **Current Rank:** ________________ **Site:** ________________ **Date:** __ __/__ __/06

In collaboration with the National Alliance for the Mentally Ill (NAMI) Maine, Center for Health Policy, Planning and Research (CHPPR) of the University of New England is conducting an evaluation of the CIT Program in your facility. We are interested in learning about your experiences and knowledge with mental health disorders. ***Your participation is voluntary and your responses will be kept confidential. CHPPR will not release participants' names.*** *Accurate and complete information is necessary to determine the impact of the program. For all questions, please choose only one response. Please mail the completed survey to CHPPR in the attached envelope. Please contact CHPPR at (207)221-4560 if you have any questions. We would like to thank you for your cooperation.*

	To what extent do you agree or disagree with the following statements:	Strongly Agree	Somewhat Agree	Neither Agree Nor Disagree	Somewhat Disagree	Strongly Disagree
1.	When someone has a mental illness, their brain is impaired in a way that effects their behavior and emotions.	☐	☐	☐	☐	☐
2.	When someone is paranoid and believes the FBI is out to get them, it is best to play along with them to get them to do what you want.	☐	☐	☐	☐	☐
3.	Most people who have mental illness had poor parenting as children.	☐	☐	☐	☐	☐
4.	In between episodes, people with a mental illness can think and feel pretty much like other people who are not ill.	☐	☐	☐	☐	☐
5.	One of the main causes of mental illness is a lack of self-discipline and will-power.	☐	☐	☐	☐	☐
6.	The best way to deal with people in mental health crisis is to set firm limits and make it clear that the officers are in charge.	☐	☐	☐	☐	☐
7.	I am comfortable in my encounters with people displaying signs of mental illness.	☐	☐	☐	☐	☐
8.	I am confident in my ability to recognize signs and symptoms of mental illness in people.	☐	☐	☐	☐	☐
9.	I am adequately trained to de-escalate a crisis situation.	☐	☐	☐	☐	☐
10.	I am confident in my ability to recognize aggression at an early stage.	☐	☐	☐	☐	☐
11.	I am confident in my ability to defuse aggression before it becomes violence (verbal de-escalation).	☐	☐	☐	☐	☐

		Yes	No	Don't Know
12.	In your view, is mental illness a biological process?	☐	☐	☐
13.	Do you understand how people develop a mental illness?	☐	☐	☐
14.	Do you know of anyone among your friends or family who has a mental health problem or a mental illness, including depression?	☐	☐	NA
15.	About how many encounters with mentally ill people in crisis have you had in the past 30 days?	_____ # of Encounters		

	For the following statements please rate your level of preparation:	Very well prepared	Moderately well prepared	Somewhat prepared	Not at all prepared
16.	How well prepared do you feel when handling people with mental illness in crisis?	☐	☐	☐	☐
17.	Overall, how well prepared do you think the other officers in your department are to handle people with mental illness in crisis?	☐	☐	☐	☐
18.	To what extent do you feel you are prepared to address a person threatening to commit suicide?	☐	☐	☐	☐

		Very effective	Moderately effective	Somewhat effective	Not at all effective
19.	Overall, how effective is your department's response to handling people with mental illness in a crisis?	☐	☐	☐	☐

CHPPR CIT OFFICER QUESTIONNAIRE 0718 — Page 1 of 2 — PLEAE TURN PAGE

		Excellent	Good	Fair	Poor
20.	How would you rate your department's ability to implement a new program for improving mental health crisis response?	☐	☐	☐	☐
		Excellent	Good	Fair	Poor
21.	How would you rate the level of administrative support for the CIT program at your jail at this point in time?	☐	☐	☐	☐
		Very helpful	Moderately helpful	Somewhat helpful	Not at all Helpful
22.	How helpful are your community's mental health resources in providing assistance to you when you are handling people with mental illness in crisis?	☐	☐	☐	☐
23.	How helpful is the emergency room/hospital system in providing assistance to you when you are handling people with mental illness in crisis?	☐	☐	☐	☐

	To what extent do you agree or disagree with the following statements:	Strongly agree	Somewhat agree	Somewhat disagree	Strongly Disagree
24.	I am comfortable in working with other agencies in finding solutions to problems encountered by persons with mental illness.	☐	☐	☐	☐
25.	I am familiar with agencies in my community/jurisdiction that I can refer a mentally ill person to.	☐	☐	☐	☐
26.	My department has established relationships with local organizations to assist with a mentally ill person.	☐	☐	☐	☐
27.	Access to mental health services is adequate in my jurisdiction.	☐	☐	☐	☐
28.	Public/private community services are conveniently available to my agency to assist with substance abuse.	☐	☐	☐	☐
29.	My department's written policy/protocol adequately provides guidance for handling mental health encounters.	☐	☐	☐	☐
30.	I have someone I can count on in my agency who can support me in my work with people with mental illness in crisis.	☐	☐	☐	☐

	Please rate your satisfaction with each of the following aspects of your job.	Very Satisfied	Somewhat Satisfied	Somewhat Dissatisfied	Very Dissatisfied
31.	The meaningfulness of the work itself	☐	☐	☐	☐
32.	Recognition of work performed	☐	☐	☐	☐
33.	Administrative support	☐	☐	☐	☐
34.	Interpersonal relationships with co-workers	☐	☐	☐	☐
35.	Adequate training for job responsibilities	☐	☐	☐	☐
36.	Working relationship with your supervisor	☐	☐	☐	☐
37.	Skills and knowledge to resolve inmate crises	☐	☐	☐	☐
38.	Overall job satisfaction	☐	☐	☐	☐

	Please rate your impressions of CIT.	Very Satisfied	Somewhat Satisfied	Somewhat Dissatisfied	Very Dissatisfied
39	How satisfied are you with the CIT training you received?	☐	☐	☐	☐
40.	How satisfied are you with the way the CIT training has prepared you to respond to handling people with mental illness in crisis?	☐	☐	☐	☐
41.	How satisfied are you with the way the CIT has been implemented at your facility?	☐	☐	☐	☐

42. What is your gender? ☐ Male ☐ Female

43. What is your age? ______ Years

44. How many years have you served as a Corrections Officer? ______ Years

45. How many years have you served at this facility? ______ Years

CHPPR CIT OFFICER QUESTIONNAIRE 0718 Page 2 of 2

CIT Police Procedures: Interacting with the Mentally Ill

Sample adapted from the Cary, North Carolina, Police Department Procedures

The (Agency) employees will provide individuals suspected of suffering from mental illness with the same high level of service and protection provided to anyone else. Reasonable procedural adjustments may be made to accommodate individual needs on a case-by-case basis. Individuals will not be taken involuntarily into custody by reason of mental illness alone, but only if they have committed an arrestable offense or have demonstrated by their actions to be a threat to the life or safety of themselves or others.

The (Agency) will restrain and transport persons in need of emergency mental commitment and those named in involuntary commitment orders to an appropriate mental health facility for evaluation. The Department will provide transportation, when manpower permits, for individuals who wish to commit themselves to a mental facility. A sworn officer will perform all mental commitments.

Definitions

- *Mental illness* – For the present purpose (CIT), mental illness is a condition that lessens the capacity of an individual to exercise self-control, judgment, and discretion in the conduct of his or her affairs and social relations to the degree that it's necessary or advisable for the person to be under treatment, care, supervision, guidance, or control.
- *Mental commitment* – For the present purpose (CIT), mental commitment is taking custody of and transporting an individual in need of and to mental health evaluation and treatment.
- *Involuntary emergency commitment* – For the present purpose (CIT), an involuntary emergency commitment is the commitment of a mental health consumer executed by an officer without a commitment order on file.
- *Involuntary non-emergency commitment* – For the present purpose (CIT), an involuntary non-emergency commitment is the commitment of a mental health consumer executed by an officer in accordance with an involuntary commitment order issued by a magistrate or clerk of court.

- *Voluntary commitment* – For the present purpose (CIT), a voluntary commitment of a mental health consumer is the commitment of a person who independently and personally decides on admission to a treatment facility.
- *24-hour facility* – A 24-hour facility is one that provides a structured living environment and services for a period of 24 consecutive hours or more.

Employee Training

All employees will receive training on how to interact with individuals suspected of suffering from mental illness. Entry-level personnel will receive documented training during new-employee orientation. Refresher training will be provided to all employees at least every three years.

Recognition of the Characteristics of Mental Illness

When called upon to interact with an individual exhibiting abnormal behavior suspected of being symptomatic of mental illness, recognition of the characteristics of mental illness may help employees decide on an appropriate response. Symptomatic behavior should be evaluated within the total context of the situation when attempting to determine an individual's mental state and the need for intervention. Guidelines for recognition of the symptoms of mental illness will be provided in employee training.

Procedures for Accessing Resources

Communications personnel will have ready access to referral information for available community mental health resources and authorized emergency evaluation facilities and will, upon request, provide this information to employees or citizens. During training, employees will familiarize themselves with procedures for accessing available community mental health resources.

Guidelines for Responding

When responding to individuals who exhibit symptoms of mental illness, employees should gather as much information as possible to assess and stabilize the situation. Specific guidelines for dealing with individuals who are suspected of suffering from mental illness will be provided in employee training.

No individual will be arrested for behavioral manifestations of mental illness that are not criminal in nature. Taking a mentally ill individual into custody can occur only when the individual has committed a crime or presents a danger to the safety of himself/herself or others and meets the criteria for involuntary emergency or non-emergency mental commitment.

Crisis Intervention Team

The (Agency) Crisis Intervention Team (CIT) works in partnership with public safety communications, health professionals, and the community to reach the common goals of safety, understanding, knowledge, and service to individuals who are in crisis and who exhibit symptoms of mental illness. Officers on the Crisis Intervention Team receive specialized training and are certified to work with mentally ill individuals and their families.

When responding to individuals who exhibit symptoms of mental illness, employees should use the Crisis Intervention Team as a resource. Whenever possible, a member of the Crisis Intervention Team should be dispatched to calls for service involving mentally ill individuals. The first Crisis Intervention Team member on the scene will assume responsibility for the call. Additional officers on the scene will provide backup as necessary. Following each call, the Crisis Intervention Team member will submit a report to the Crisis Intervention Team Coordinator.

Commitment Procedures

Involuntary Emergency Commitment

Any person subject to involuntary commitment due to mental illness and who requires immediate hospitalization to prevent harm to him-/herself or others will be taken into immediate custody and restrained in an appropriate manner.

The officer will then transport the person to (Name) County Human Services/ Emergency Admissions for evaluation.

If inpatient treatment is recommended, the officer will transport the person to (name the 24-hour facility) for the second evaluation. If, upon the second evaluation, the examining psychiatrist finds that the person requires inpatient treatment, the officer will transfer custody to hospital personnel. If the examining psychiatrist recommends outpatient treatment, the officer will transport the person back to his or her residence or to the home of a consenting individual.

In the event that the examining psychiatrist finds no evidence of mental illness, the person will be released and the proceedings terminated. If the person so desires, the officer will provide transportation back to the person's residence.

Involuntary Non-Emergency Commitment

Once the officer has verified that an order for involuntary commitment is on file, the officer will take the subject of that order into custody and restrain the person in an appropriate manner with reasonable force. If the officer does not have the actual order in his possession when the person is taken into custody, he must obtain the order before the person is transported to (name the 24-hour facility) Human Services/Emergency Admissions for examination.

If the examining psychiatrist recommends inpatient treatment, the officer will transport the person to the 24-hour facility specified on the commitment order. If a hospital outside of the county is selected and it's not within reasonable driving distance, the officer will notify the sheriff's office to conduct the transport and the officer will remain with the patient until relieved by hospital staff or a sheriff's deputy. If the selected hospital is within reasonable driving distance, the officer will transport the person to the facility. If outpatient treatment is recommended, the officer will return the completed commitment order to the magistrate's office and transport the person back to the person's residence or to the home of a consenting individual.

Upon arrival at (name the 24-hour facility) or other specified facility, the officer will wait up to one hour for the person to be examined. If the person has not been examined by the end of that hour, the officer will notify the appropriate attending medical personnel that the person will be left in the custody of hospital personnel. The officer will then return the signed original commitment order to the magistrate's office.

In the event the person is hospitalized and the involuntary commitment order has been issued by a magistrate based on the attending physician's initial examination and affidavit, the officer will assist in transporting the patient to the hospital named on the commitment order, provided that the hospital is within reasonable driving distance. Transport of the patient will be by ambulance and will be scheduled by (name the hospital or facility). The officer will ride in the ambulance with the patient and the paramedic team. Upon turning over custody of the patient to the hospital staff, the officer will notify an on-duty supervisor to arrange transportation back to his or her patrol vehicle. Then the officer will return the served order to the magistrate's office.

When transporting a female patient from (name the hospital or facility), at least one member of the transport team must be female.

Voluntary Commitment

The Department will provide transportation, if staffing levels permit, for individuals wishing to commit themselves to a mental institution. If no one is available to transport the individual, the Department will make every reasonable effort to locate an alternative source of transportation

Transportation of Persons Subject to Evaluation

An officer of the same sex will provide transportation for persons subject to mental health evaluation unless a family member of the person accompanies the person during transport.

The preferred option is to have a family member accompany the patient. The second option, if necessary, is to call in a sworn employee of the Department who is the same sex as the person being transported. As a last resort, the officer may be accompanied by a non-sworn employee of the Department or an available professional.

CIT Memorandum of Understanding

Sample MOU between a County Mental Health Department and CIT Community Partners: Adapted from the North Carolina Five County Mental Health Authority MOU

THIS AGREEMENT is made and entered into this ____ day of ___________, 20xx, between _____________ (name the law enforcement dept.), the National Alliance on Mental Illness (NAMI), and _________________ (name the mental health agency), hereafter referred to as Parties:

WHEREAS, the above-named Parties endeavor and agree to prevent—when possible—the arrest and incarceration of people with mental illness and effectively link these individuals to appropriate mental health treatment in the community:

NOW, THEREFORE, it is agreed in consideration of the mutual promises set forth herein that (name the responsible agency) CIT will emphasize the training of specially selected law enforcement officers with skills and knowledge about mental illness to respond to crisis situations involving people with mental illness.

The (name the responsible agency) and contracted providers will provide rapid assessment and referral to appropriate mental health community services and support for people with mental illness requiring law enforcement involvement. In addition, the Parties agree to work cooperatively to do the following:

- Recognize that CIT begins with law enforcement professionals who are the first on the scene and must make the right decisions for people with mental illness.
- Emphasize that CIT officers will be expeditiously afforded as much support as advocates, service providers, and the community can afford.
- Emphasize treatment rather than incarceration of people with mental illness.
- Decrease the proportion of people with mental illness in county jails.
- Prevent the inappropriate incarceration and/or criminalization of people with mental illness.
- Improve and minimize the turnaround time for law enforcement officers who have custody of a person suffering mental illness.

- Decrease officer injury rates.
- Decrease injury rates to persons experiencing a mental health crisis requiring law enforcement involvement.
- Increase law enforcement officers' knowledge about mental illness and skills in their interactions with people with mental illness.
- Provide training to selected law enforcement officers.
- Improve the relationships between mental health service providers and law enforcement departments.
- Participate in evaluation of the (name the responsible agency) CIT process, goals, and outcome measures.

This Agreement shall continue in effect from the date entered into for a period of one (1) year. Upon the expiration of said period, this Agreement shall be automatically renewed for an additional one (1) year term unless notice of termination is received by any party within thirty (30) days prior to the expiration of any term.

____________________________________ Date ____________________
National Alliance on Mental Illness (NAMI)

____________________________________ Date ____________________
(Law Enforcement Agency)

____________________________________ Date ____________________

(Name the responsible agency)
Mental Health Authority

CIT Law Enforcement Officer Policy

Crisis Intervention Team

The (name the Police/Sheriff's Departments) Crisis Intervention Team (CIT) works to decriminalize the mentally ill. It does this by working to establish partnerships with public safety communications and health professionals and community mental health consumer advocates to reach the common goals of safety, understanding, knowledge, and service to individuals who are in crisis and who exhibit symptoms of mental illness. Officers on the CIT receive specialized training and are certified to work with mentally ill individuals and their families to resolve the issue at the lowest level possible. While arrest is possible, it should be resorted to only if all other avenues for resolution have been exhausted.

When responding to individuals who exhibit symptoms of mental illness, responding officers should use the CIT-trained officer as a resource. Whenever possible, a member of the CIT should be initially dispatched to calls for service involving mentally ill individuals. The first CIT member on the scene will assume responsibility for the call. Additional officers on the scene will provide backup as necessary. Following each call, the CIT member will submit a report to the (name the party responsible for data collection and reporting).

Refer to your departmental policy to ensure this meets the necessary mandates.

CIT Mobile Crisis Management Fact Sheet

Courtesy of Integrated Family Services, PLLC, North Carolina

What does the mobile crisis management services team do?

The mobile crisis management services team provides integrated crisis response, crisis stabilization, and crisis prevention activities. The service is available 24/7/365. Crisis response provides immediate evaluation, triage, and access to acute mental health, developmental disabilities, and substance abuse services and support. The team designs prevention strategies to reduce the incidence of recurring crises. If the recipient has a current mental health provider, he or she will develop or modify crisis plans to assist with crisis prevention.

What defines a crisis?

The definition of a crisis differs depending on who is defining it. However, in the context of providing services, a crisis is any situation that causes a person to deviate from his/her normal level of functioning, with a lack of coping skills to handle the situation.

How is someone qualified to receive mobile crisis management services?

Priority should be given to individuals with a history of multiple crisis episodes and/or who are at substantial risk of future crises. The following factors are considered:

- *Immediacy* – The person (and/or family) is experiencing an acute, immediate crisis.
- *Limited resources* – The person (and/or family) has insufficient or severely limited resources or skills necessary to cope with the immediate crisis.
- *Impaired judgment* – The person evidences impairment of judgment and/or impulse control and/or cognitive/perceptual disabilities.
- *Under the influence* – The person is intoxicated or in withdrawal and in need of substance abuse treatment and unable to access services without immediate assistance.

Who is eligible for mobile crisis management services?

All citizens within (name jurisdictions) are eligible to receive mobile crisis services.

Are clients with current mental health providers eligible to receive mobile crisis management services?

The mobile crisis management service is a second-level service, which means that the mental health provider should (especially those that respond with the CIT officer to a call for service) provide the first response in a crisis situation. If a provider needs additional assistance to stabilize the crisis situation, the mobile crisis team can respond with the understanding that mobile crisis will bill for reimbursement for the service provided. It is expected by the Local Management Entity that mental health providers will utilize this service and incorporate it into the client's crisis plan as a resource. If an established client receives mobile crisis management services, the team must review the client's crisis plan to determine what strategies did not work and make changes as necessary.

Does a recipient of mobile crisis management services have to have insurance coverage?

All recipients are eligible to receive mobile crisis management services regardless of their insurance coverage.

Where are mobile crisis management services provided?

Mobile crisis management services are provided in least restrictive settings (homes, schools, doctor's offices, stores, law enforcement facilities, and the like).

What is the response time once a call is received by the mobile crisis team?

The state service definition indicates that the Integrated Family Services (IFS) mobile crisis team has one hour to make telephone contact and two hours to make face-to-face contact.

What credentials do the mobile crisis management team members have?

The mobile crisis management team has 24-hour access to a psychiatrist for consultation. The team consists of a licensed clinical social worker (LCSW), qualified professionals with experience with developmental disabilities, a certified substance abuse counselor/certified clinical addiction specialist/certified clinical supervisor and paraprofessionals or associate professionals with supervision. All team members have a minimum of one-year experience working with people in crisis.

What is the program structure of the IFS Mobile Crisis Team?

The mobile crisis supervisor or mobile crisis worker responds to calls received during the day. After office hours, on the weekends, and on holidays, coverage is maintained by an on-call rotation. All team members report to the LCSW on the team.

How can referrals be made to the mobile crisis management team?

All referral sources should call (add appropriate phone number) to report their crisis situation.

What are possible referral sources?

Department of Social Services, Department of Juvenile Justice Delinquency Prevention, Criminal Justice system, private providers, schools, individuals, crisis lines, etc.

What are the benefits of using mobile crisis management services?

- Decriminalization of the mental health consumer via jail diversion
- Keeping clients in the community
- Mobility in rural areas
- Alternative to hospitalization
- Linkage to services and resources that could de-escalate a crisis situation
- Early intervention

CIT Program Resources and Key Contacts

Discovering how to go about your program is a matter of selecting those few things that make your idea possible, practical, and potent. Resources make it possible. Good advice from experienced program stakeholders will make your program doable. Focusing on the particular activities and resources that make your idea an answer to local needs will make it socially transformative.[80]

Resources from the Web
https://csgjusticecenter.org/mental-health/resources/ (Viewed July 17, 2024) – The **Criminal Justice/Mental Health Information Network.** The InfoNet is coordinated by the Criminal Justice/Mental Health Consensus Program and the CMHS National GAINS Center, with invaluable support from the National Alliance on Mental Illness (NAMI) and other organizations. Content on the site, which is still being developed, is organized and searchable using the components of the criminal justice and mental health systems, which courts, corrections, and community support. See this list of resources:
https://www.theiacp.org/sites/default/files/2018-08/2009SummitUsefulResources.pdf (Viewed July 17, 2024)

https://csgjusticecenter.org/ (Viewed July 17, 2024) – The **Council of State Governments** is a national nonprofit organization that serves policymakers at the local, state, and federal levels from all branches of government. It provides practical, nonpartisan advice and consensus-driven strategies, informed by available evidence, to increase public safety and strengthen communities. For example, it designed and conducted the Consensus Program to help mental health consumers.

http://csgjusticecenter.org/mental-health (Viewed July 17, 2024) – **The Consensus Program** is a national effort to provide information, research, and support to organizations attempting to help people with mental illness in the criminal justice system. It's sponsored by the Council of State Governments.

https://nami.org/Get-Involved/Crisis-Intervention-Team-(CIT)-Programs/CIT-Resources (Viewed July 17, 2024) – **NAMI (National Alliance on Mental Illness)** provides a number of resources regarding CIT. Search for CIT on *https://nami.org*

and you'll find others. The NAMI CIT Technical Assistance Resource Center has information for law enforcement, advocacy, and mental health workers, and consumers regarding Crisis Intervention Team (CIT) training. It serves as a repository of information about CIT programs nationwide. The Center facilitates ongoing communications between CIT programs and engages in national networking to establish standards and promote the expansion of CIT.

https://www.samhsa.gov/ (Viewed July 17, 2024) – The **SAMHSA Health Information Network** (SHIN) connects the behavioral health workforce and the general public to the latest information on the prevention and treatment of mental and substance use disorders.

https://rapidsos.com/why-the-vitals-app-became-rapidsos-ready/ (Viewed July 17, 2024) – "T**he Vitals™ app** is a life-saving technology designed to bridge the communication gap between first responders and individuals living with invisible or visible conditions and disabilities – delivering greater peace of mind for everyone."

Funding

Funding is important for the support of dedicated CIT officers and coordinators, either full time or part-time. The best funding is a mix of funding sources: both soft (grants, donations, and giving) and hard (a budget line item).

A lucrative, though not easy, route is to develop a plan that extends from small donations to large corporate gifts and even estate bequests.

Development is the work of years. The more requests for funding you make the easier it becomes and the more successes you have. The first application is the toughest, but it's the basic template for the next application, which will be better than its predecessor.

Following are sources to consider.

https://bja.ojp.gov/funding/current (Viewed July 17, 2024) – The **Bureau of Justice Assistance (BJA)** in Washington, DC, is a source for funding for local service programs. It supports law enforcement, courts, corrections, treatment, victim services, technology, and prevention initiatives that strengthen the nation's criminal justice system. Just be aware that any grant, especially from the feds is highly competitive, fraught with rules, regulations, and oversight—and terminal. Grants usually expire just when a program gets established. The BJA also provides information on allowable program activities and funding cycles for the Byrne Memorial Grant, which is amenable to CIT ideas. ***https://bja.ojp.gov/program/jag/overview*** (Viewed July 18, 2024)

BJA provides leadership, services, and funding to America's communities by:

- Emphasizing local control.
- Building relationships in the field.
- Providing training and technical assistance in support of efforts to prevent crime, drug abuse, and violence at the national, state, and local levels.
- Developing collaborations and partnerships.
- Promoting Capacity Building through planning.
- Streamlining the administration of grants.
- Increasing training and technical assistance.
- Creating accountability of programs.
- Encouraging innovation.
- Communicating the value of justice efforts to decision makers at every level.

https://ojp.gov/funding/index.htm (Viewed July 18, 2024) – **The U.S. Department of Justice, Office of Justice Program**s has a Funding Resource Center where you can explore funding opportunities and receive technical assistance.

https://www.ncjrs.gov/ (Viewed July 18, 2024) – **The National Criminal Justice Reference Service (NCJRS)** is the clearinghouse for BJA. It offers a range of services and resources, balancing the information needs of the field with the technological means to receive and access support.

Also refer to the U.S. Department of Justice Response Center for questions and concerns: 1-800-458-0786.

https://ojp.gov/about/offices/customer_service.htm (Viewed July 18, 2024)

Most agencies have relevant solicitations, while the competition is stiff. Some agencies you may not have thought to consider are:

[https://www.]

- ***cms.gov/*** – Centers for Medicare and Medicaid Services
- ***hhs.gov/*** – The Department of Health and Human Services
- ***hud.gov/*** – The Department of Housing and Urban Development
- ***samhsa.gov*** – The Substance Abuse and Mental Health Services Administration
- ***ssa.gov*** – The Social Security Administration
- ***va.gov*** – The Department of Veterans Affairs

https://www.samhsa.gov/gains-center (Viewed July 18, 2024) – **The GAINS Center** focuses on expanding access to services for people with mental and/or substance use disorders who come into contact with the justice system. SAMHSA makes grant funds available through the Center for Substance Abuse Prevention, the Center for Substance Abuse Treatment, and the Center for Mental Health Services. Find funding opportunities that support programs for substance use disorders and mental illness, and learn about the grant application, review, and management process. ***https://www.samhsa.gov/grants*** (Viewed July 18, 2024)

https://candid.org/ (Viewed July 18, 2024) – **Candid** provides a comprehensive set of resources for locating and approaching foundations.

Consider public, private, private nonprofit sectors, and donations for funding. It's wise when developing any local service idea to develop contacts and expertise at all three levels of government as well as private and nonprofit sources.

- *Federal* – At the Federal level, investigate ***https://www.grants.gov.*** This might be a source for further funding of an existing CIT program. For example, an existing program may seek a federal grant source for an enhanced CIT program. Realistically, it's a tough source to pursue, but funding is a game of numbers; the more attempts the more the successes.
- *State* – At the state level, you'll have a single point of contact, usually at the governor's office or a state administrative agency (SAA, responsible for block grant administration), which is charged with distributing grant funds. Perhaps develop a CIT-relevant, one-page proposal/concept to present to these agencies for sub-granting.
- *Local* – At the local level, a good tactic is to justify a hardline item in the budget for your program.
- *Private* – In the private sector, businesses usually support community programs as part of their mission. You need to present a good business proposal that justifies giving to your program.
- *Nonprofit* – Foundations are also eager to hear a good proposal for giving. However, they usually require a highly detailed application and may take months before they announce awards. The Duke Endowment

(https://dukeendowment.org/), which supports issues of community partnership, and the Kate B. Reynolds Charitable Trust *(www.KBR.org)* have proven useful sources for mental illness community programs in the Carolinas. (Viewed July 18, 2024)

Organizations

https://www.nasmhpd.org/ (Viewed July 18, 2024) – **National Association of State Mental Health Program Directors.** This website is especially useful for finding links to mental health organizations and information sources.

Program Examples

http://cit.memphis.edu (Viewed July 18, 2024) – **The University of Memphis CIT Center** is a good CIT resource as it was the original model and has over two decades of experience in decriminalizing the mentally ill.

https://www.memphispolice.org (Viewed July 18, 2024) – The **Crisis Investigation Bureau of the Memphis Police Department** is the repository for the corporate knowledge for the Memphis Model.

http://www.naco.org/sites/default/files/documents/Jail%20Diversion%20Toolkit.pdf (Viewed July 18, 2024) – The Bexar County, Texas, **"Blueprint for Success: The Bexar County Model – How to Set up a Jail Diversion Program in Your Community"** makes the case for a comprehensive network of pre- and post-booking solutions to decriminalizing the mentally ill, including what can be done within the courts, jails, law enforcement, and mental health services.

www.houstoncit.org (Viewed July 18, 2024) – The **Houston Police Department** has the largest CIT program in the nation at the time of this writing. This site provides examples of all the various CIT activities associated with a well-established CIT program.

Publications

Bayne, W. C. "Furor Sparks Call for Crisis Team," *Commercial Appeal*, B1-B2. Memphis, Tennessee, 30 September 1987.

Borum, R. "Improving High Risk Encounters Between People with Mental Illness and Police," *Journal of the American Academy of Psychiatry and the Law,* 2000, 28, 332-33.

Borum, R., M. W. Deane, H. J. Steadman, & J. Morrissey. "Police Perspectives on Responding to Mentally Ill People in Crisis: Perceptions of Program Effectiveness." *Behavioral Sciences and the Law,* 1998, 16, 393-405.

Clay, R. "Jail Diversion Programs Enhance Care," *SAMHSA News,* 2000, Spring, VIII (2), 1-5.

Cochran, S. "The Crisis Intervention Team Model in Action," *Community Mental Health Report,* 2000, 2, 31.

Compton, M. T., M. L. Esterberg, R. McGee, R. J. Kotwicki, & J. R. Oliva. "Brief Reports: Crisis Intervention Team Training: Changes in Knowledge, Attitudes, and Stigma Related to Schizophrenia," *Psychiatric Services*, 2006, 57, 1199-1202.

Compton, Michael T., M. Bahora, Amy C. Watson, Janet R. Oliva. "A Comprehensive Review of Extant Research on Crisis Intervention Team (CIT) Programs," *Journal of the American Academy of Psychiatry and the Law,* 2008, 36, 47-55.

Cowell, A., N. Broner, & R. Dupont. "The Cost-Effectiveness of Criminal Justice Diversion Programs for People with Serious Mental Illness Co-Occurring with Substance Abuse: Four Case Studies." *Journal of Contemporary Criminal Justice,* 2004, 20, 292-314.

Dank, N. R., & M. Kulishoff. "An Alternative to the Incarceration of the Mentally Ill," *Journal of Prison and Jail Health,* 1993, 3, 95-100.

Dowd, J. "Crossing the Line: Formal Training Can Transform Relations Between the Police and Mental Health Services," *Mental Health Today,* 2004, 4, 14-15.

Dupont, R. "The Crisis Intervention Team Model: An Intersection Point for the Criminal Justice System and the Psychiatric Emergency Service," 2008. In R.

Glick et al. *Emergency Psychiatry: Principles and Practice,* 381-392. Philadelphia: Lippincott, Williams & Williams, 2004.

Dupont, R. "How the Crisis Intervention Team Model Enhances Policing and Improves Community Mental Health," *Community Health Report,* 2001, 2(1), 3-4.

Dupont, R. & S. Cochran. "Police Response to Mental Health Emergencies: Barriers to Change," *The Journal of the American Academy of Psychiatry and the Law,* 2000, 28, 338-344.

Finn, P. E. & M. Sullivan. "Police Handling of the Mentally Ill: Sharing Responsibility with the Mental Health System," *Journal of Criminal Justice,* 1989, 17, 1-14.

Gentz, D. & W. Goree. "Moving Past What to How: The Next Step in Responding to Individuals with Mental Illness." *FBI Law Enforcement Bulletin,* 2003, 72(11), 14-18.

Green, T. "Police as Frontline Mental Health Workers: The Decision to Arrest or Refer to Mental Health Agencies," International Journal of Law and Psychiatry, 1987, 20, 469-486.

Hill, R. "Civil Liability and Mental Illness: A Proactive Model to Mitigate Claims," *The Police Chief,* 2001.

Lattimore, P. K., N. Broner, R. Sherman, L. Frisman, & M. S. Shafer. "A Comparison of Pre-Booking and Post-Booking Diversion Programs for Mentally Ill Substance-Using Individuals with Justice Involvement," *Journal of Contemporary Criminal Justice,* 2003, 19, 30-64. Describes eight programs representing a variety of approaches to diversion in terms of point of criminal justice intervention (pre-booking or post-booking), degree of criminal justice coercion, type of linkages provided to community-based treatment, and approaches to treatment retention.

Munetz, M. R. & P. A. Griffin. "Use of the Sequential Intercept Model as an Approach to Decriminalization of People with Serious Mental Illness," *Psychiatric Services,* 2006, April, Vol. 57, No. 4, 544-549.

Reuland, M. *A Guide to Implementing Police-Based Diversion Programs for People with Mental Illness.* Delmar, NY: Technical Assistance and Policy Analysis Center for Jail Diversion, 2004.

Reuland, M. and G. Margolis. "Police Approaches That Improve the Response to People with Mental Illnesses: A Focus on Victims" (electronic version), *The Police Chief,* 2003, 70(11), 35-39.

Reuland, M., L. Draper & B. Norton. *Improving Responses to People with Mental Illnesses: Tailoring Law Enforcement Initiatives to Individual Jurisdictions,* Council of State Governments Justice Center and the Police Executive Research Forum for the Bureau of Justice Assistance, Office of Justice Programs, U.S. Department of Justice, Washington, DC, 2010.

Skeem, J. & B. Lynne. "How Does Violence Potential Relate to Crisis Intervention Team Responses to Emergencies?" *Psychiatric Services,* 2008, 59:201-204.

Steadman, H. J., J. J. Cocozza, B. M. Veysey. "Comparing Outcomes for Diverted and Non-Diverted Jail Detainees with Mental Illness," *Law and Human Behavior,* 1999, 23, 615-627.

Steadman, H. J., M. W. Deane, R. Borum, & J. P. Morrissey. "Comparing Outcomes of Major Models of Police Responses to Mental Health Emergencies," *Psychiatric Services,* 2000, 51, 645-649. This study compared three models of police responses to incidents involving people thought to have mental illnesses to determine how often specialized professionals responded and how often they were able to resolve cases without arrest. Conclusions: Data strongly suggest that collaborations between the criminal justice system, the mental health system, and the advocacy community plus essential services reduce the inappropriate use of U.S. jails to house persons with acute symptoms of mental illness.

Strauss, G., M. Glenn, P. Reddi, I. Afaq, A. Podolskaya, T. Rybakova, et al. "Psychiatric Disposition of Patients Brought in by Crisis Intervention Team Police Officers," *Community Mental Health Journal,* 2005, 41, 223-228. Conclusions: CIT officers appear to do a good job at identifying patients in need of psychiatric care.

Teller, J. L. S., M. R. Munetz, K. M. Gil, & C. Ritter. "Crisis Intervention Team Training for Police Officers Responding to Mental Disturbance Calls," *Psychiatric Services,* 2006, 57, 232-237.

Teplin, L. "Police Discretion and Persons with Mental Illness," *Community Mental Health Report,* 2001, 1, 37-38, 45-46.

Teplin, L. & N. Pruett. "Police as Street Corner Psychiatrist: Managing the Mentally Ill," *International Journal of Law and Psychiatry,* 1992, 15, 139-156.

Walsh, J. & D. Holt. "Jail Diversion for People with Psychiatric Disabilities: The Sheriff's Perspective," *Psychiatric Rehabilitation Journal,* 1999, 23, 153-160.

Watson, A. C., P. W. Corrigan, & V. Ottati. "Police Officers' Attitudes Toward and Decisions about Persons with Mental Illness," *Psychiatric Services,* 2004, 55, 49-53.

Woody, M. "The Art of De-escalation," *The Journal,* 2005, Summer, 26-62. Retrieved July 17, 2006, from Northeastern Ohio University College of Medicine Division of Clinical Sciences.

Services

https://mentalhealthrecovery.com/ (Viewed July 18, 2024) – This site features emerging evidence-based practices in mental health services and features WRAP, or the **Wellness Recovery Action Plan,** for prevention and well-being.

www.cmhsrp.uic.edu/nrtc (Viewed July 18, 2024) – T**he National Research and Training Center on Psychiatric Disability (NRTC)** promotes access to effective consumer-driven and community-based services for adults with serious mental illness. The Center is located at the University of Illinois at Chicago in the Department of Psychiatry.

Strategic Planning

https://ojp.gov/ncjrs/virtual-library/abstracts/improving-responses-people-mental-illnesses-essential-elements-0 (Viewed July 18, 2024) – "Improving Responses to People with Mental Illnesses: Essential Elements of a Mental Health

Court" is a report sponsored by the Bureau of Justice Assistance (BJA). It provides an overview of the benefits of mental health courts should your jail diversion program consider diversion via the courts. Note that CIT pre-booking with a mental health court plus a jail diversion program constitutes a comprehensive approach to jail diversion.

https://csgjusticecenter.org/publications/law-enforcement-responses-to-people-with-mental-illnesses-a-guide-to-research-informed-policy-and-practice/ (Viewed July 18, 2024) – "Law Enforcement Responses to People With Mental Illness: A Guide to Research-Informed Policy and Practice" provides an overview of specialized responses to the mentally ill. A PDF download on the site of The Council of State Governments Justice Center.

http://cit.memphis.edu/CoreElements.pdf (Viewed July 18, 2024) – "Crisis Intervention Team Core Elements" suggests some critical milestones for planning a CIT effort.

https://csgjusticecenter.org/publications/collaboration-assessment-tool/ (Viewed July 18, 2024) – The Criminal Justice/ Mental Health Consensus Program's **Collaboration Assessment Tool.**

Training

https://jmhcp.org/ (Viewed July 18, 2024) – **Justice and Mental Health Collaboration Program.** "From first contact to reentry, the Justice and Mental Health Collaboration Program (JMHCP) supports criminal justice and behavioral health systems across the country as they safely divert people from the justice system and increase access to mental health treatment, innovative crisis services, housing supports, and more."

Murphy, G. *Managing Persons with Mental Disabilities: A Curriculum Guide for Police Trainers*. Washington, D.C.: Police Executive Research Forum, 1989.

REFERENCES

Bexar County, Texas, "Blueprint for Success: The Bexar County Model – How to Set up a Jail Diversion Program in Your Community" *http://www.naco.org/sites/default/files/documents/Jail%20Diversion%20Toolkit.pdf* (Viewed July 18, 2024)

Callahan, K. & K. Kloby. "Moving Toward Outcome-Oriented Performance Measurement Systems," Managing for Performance and Results Series, IBM Center for The Business of Government, Washington, DC, 2009.

Center for Health Policy, Planning and Research. "Crisis Intervention Team (CIT) Training for Correctional Officers," 2007, viewed 14 May 2012. No longer available. See *www.nami.org* for the latest articles.

Cissner, A. & D. J. Farole, Jr.. "Avoiding Failures of Implementation: Lessons from Process Evaluations," Center for Court Innovation and The Bureau of Justice Assistance, Washington, D.C., 2009. *https://www.courtinnovation.org/publications/avoiding-failures-implementation-lessons-process-evaluations* (Viewed July 18, 2024)

Council of State Governments, "Criminal Justice/Mental Health Consensus Project," 2002, viewed 6 May 2019. *https://csgjusticecenter.org/wp-content/uploads/2013/03/consensus-project-full-report.pdf*

Dupont, R., S. Cochran, & S. Pillsbury. "Crisis Intervention Team Core Elements," The University of Memphis, School of Public Policy, Department of Criminology and Criminal Justice, CIT Center, 2007. *http://cit.memphis.edu/pdf/CoreElements.pdf* (Viewed July 18, 2024)

Frontline, "The New Asylums," PBS, 10 May 2005, viewed 7 May 2019. *http://www.pbs.org/wgbh/pages/frontline/shows/asylums/etc/synopsis.html*

Gladwell, M. "Million-Dollar Murray: Why Problems Like Homelessness May Be Easier to Solve Than to Manage," *The New Yorker*, iss. 02-13 and 20, 2006.

Hoina, C. "Crisis Intervention Teams (CIT) in North Carolina: A Template for Success," unpublished consulting guide, 2010.

Hoina, C., Lt., retired, Cary N.C. Police Department. Interview 1 July 2013.

Honberg, R. & D. Gruttadaro. "Flawed Mental Health Policies and The Tragedy of Criminalization," *Corrections Today*, vol. 67, February 2005.

Imas, K. "Stopping the Revolving Door," State News, The Council of State Governments 2005. *http://www.csg.org* (Viewed July 2, 2009)

Klopovic, J., M. Vasu & D. Yearwood. *Effective Program Practices for At-Risk Youth: A Continuum of Community Based Programs,* Civic Research Institute, New York, NY, 2003.

Lamb, H., L. Weinberger & W. DeCuir. "Police and Mental Health," *Psychiatric Services,* 2002, vol. 53, 1266-1271.

Lorman Education Services. "Crisis Intervention Team Training for Law Enforcement for the 21st-Century," 2010. (Viewed September 17, 2012) Article no longer available.

Macdonald, H. "A Crime Theory Demolished," *The Wall Street Journal,* January 7, 2010.

McWilliams, E. *How to Survive Best Practice,* University of New South Wales Press Ltd., Sydney, NSW, 2002.

Munetz, M., A. Morrison, J. Krake, B. Young, & M. Woody. "State Mental Health Policy: Statewide Implementation of the Crisis Intervention Team Program: The Ohio Model," *Psychiatric Services,* 2006, vol. 57, 1569-1571.

Oliva, J. & M. Compton. "A Statewide Crisis Intervention Team (CIT) Initiative: Evolution of the Georgia CIT Program," *J Am Acad Psychiatry Law,* 2008, vol. 36:1, 38-46.

Pew, "Pew Center on the States – One in 31: The Long Reach of American Corrections," 2009. *https://www.pewtrusts.org/~/media/assets/ 2009/03/02/ pspp_1in31_report_final_web_32609.pdf.* (Viewed July 19, 2024)

Pressman, J. & A. Wildavsky. *Implementation,* University of California Press, CA, 1984.

Reuland, M. *A Guide to Implementing Police-Based Diversion Programs for People with Mental Illness,* Delmar, NY: The TAPA Center for Jail Diversion, 2004.

Reuland, M., L. Draper, & B. Norton. "Improving Responses to People with Mental Illnesses: Tailoring Law Enforcement Initiatives to Individual Jurisdictions," Council of State Governments Justice Center and the Police Executive Research Forum for the Bureau of Justice Assistance, Office of Justice Programs, U.S. Department of Justice, Washington, DC, 2010.

Rich, A. "Mental Illness and the Criminal Justice System," *State Government News,* 2002 – (Viewed July 2, 2009) *www.csg.org*

Ridgeway, J. & J. Casella. "Locking Down the Mentally Ill," 2010. (Viewed February 25, 2010) – *https://thecrimereport.org/2010/02/18/locking-down-the-mentally-ill/*

Sheehan, R. "Shuttling Patients Burdens Deputies," The News and Observer, 2010. (Viewed January 10, 2010) *https://crime.blogs.com/tre/2010/01/shuttling-patients-burdens-deputies.html*

Steadman, H. "Practical Advice on Jail Diversion: Ten Years of Learnings on Jail Diversion from the CMHS National GAINS Center," 2007. (Viewed May 14, 2012) – *http://www.pacenterofexcellence.pitt.edu/documents/PracticalAdvice OnJailDiversion.pdf*

Steadman, H. & M. Naples. "Assessing the Effectiveness of Jail Diversion Programs for Persons with Serious Mental Illness and Co-Occurring Substance Use Disorders," *Behavioral Sciences and the Law,* 2005, vol. 23, 163-170.

Steadman, H., M. Williams-Deane, J. Morrissey, M. Westcott, S. Salasin, & S. Shapiro. "A SAMHSA Research Initiative Assessing the Effectiveness of Jail Diversion Programs for Mentally Ill Persons," *Psychiatric Services,* Dec. 1999, vol. 50, no. 12.

Tremblay, J. *Towards an Integrated Network: Working Together to Avoid Criminalization of People with Mental Health Problems,* St. Leonard's Society of Canada and the Canadian Criminal Justice Association, Ottawa, ON, 2008.

Vickers, B. "Memphis, Tennessee, Police Department's Crisis Intervention Team," Practitioner Perspectives, U.S. Department of Justice, Bureau of Justice Assistance, July 2000. (Viewed July 18, 2024) – *https://www.ncjrs.gov/pdffiles1/bja/182501.pdf*

Wells, D. & L. Doherty. A Handbook for Strategic Planning, 2010. (Viewed May 14, 2012) – *http://unpan1.un.org/intradoc/groups/public/documents/ aspa/ unpan002504.pdf*

Young, A. & N. Brumley. "On-scene Mental Health Services: Establishing a Crisis Team," *FBI Law Enforcement Bulletin,* 2009, vol. 78, iss. 9, 6-11.

Attributions for Photographs and Figures

Photographs

Introduction: North Carolina Start Respite and Team, 24/7 Crisis Response. Photo courtesy of: *https://rhahealthservices.org/service-descriptions/crisis-services-north-carolina/*

Chapter 1: Durham, Ontario's Crisis Intervention Team combines a psychiatrically trained registered nurse with a CIT officer. Photo courtesy of: *https://www.durham-region.com/news-story/6229065-background-durham-s-mobile-crisis-intervention-team/*

Chapter 2: Mobile Crisis Response. Photo courtesy of: *https://www.lsbc.net/services/adult-clinical/mobile-crisis-response/*
Chapter 3: Hill Country's mobile mental health office, Redding, California. Photo courtesy of Hill Country Health and Wellness Center, Redding, CA: *https://www.redding.com/story/news/2019/01/22/hill-countrys-mobile-mental-health-crisis-team-hits-streets/2598967002/*

Chapter 4: Colorado Springs Community Response Team. Photo courtesy of: *https://www.emsworld.com/article/219668/close-colorado-springs-community-response-team*

Chapter 5: Encouraging quote on the wall inside the Yavapai County, Arizona, jail's mental health unit. Photo courtesy of Max Efrein/Courier: *http://www.verdenews.com/news/2018/feb/08/yavapai-county-decriminalizing-mental-illness/*

Figures

Fig. 1-A: CIT Capacity Building Checklist – PHASES I-III, with Key Action Items and Effective Practices (Author James Klopovic)

Appendix, Fig. 1-B: CIT Capacity Building Checklist – PHASES I-III, with Key Action Items and Effective Practices (Author James Klopovic)

Chapter 1, Fig. 2: The Sequential Intercept Model: Advancing Community-Based Solutions for Justice-Involved People with Mental and Substance Use Disorders. Policy Research Associates, Delmar, NY. *www.prainc.com/sim* (Viewed July 19, 2024)

Chapter 1, Fig. 3: Events an Individual with Mental Illness May Experience in the Criminal Justice System. Council of State Governments 2002. *https://csgjustice-center.org/publications/the-consensus-project-report/* (Viewed July 19, 2024)

ENDNOTES

1 Policy Research Associates, The Sequential Intercept Model: Advancing Community-Based Solutions for Justice-Involved People with Mental and Substance Use Disorders. Delmar, NY. *www.prainc.com/sim* (Viewed July 19, 2024)

2 J. Klopovic, M. Vasu, & D. Yearwood. *Effective Program Practices for At-Risk Youth: A Continuum of Community Based Programs,* Civic Research Institute, New York, NY, 2003.

3 Ibid.

4 R. Sheehan, "Shuttling Patients Burdens Deputies," *The News and Observer,* 2010. *https://crime.blogs.com/tre/2010/01/shuttling-patients-burdens-deputies.html* (Viewed Jan. 10, 2010)

5 Ibid.

6 B. Vickers, *Memphis Tennessee, Police Department's Crisis Intervention Team,* Bureau of Justice Assistance Clearinghouse, Rockville, MD, 2000.

7 *http://crisissolutionsnc.org/cit/(Viewed July 19, 2024, 2024)*

8 R. Gulati, "Silo Busting, How to execute on the Promise of Customer Focus" in HBR's 10 Must Reads: On collaboration, pp. 59-78, CR 2013. Harvard Business School Publishing Corporation, Boston, 2007.

9 Ibid. Adapted from Gulati, p. 61.

10 Council of State Governments, Criminal Justice/Mental Health 2002. *https://csgjusticecenter.org/publications/the-consensus-project-report/* (Viewed July 19, 2024) (See flowchart p. 25).

11 H. Steadman & M. Naples. "Assessing the Effectiveness of Jail Diversion Programs for Persons with Serious Mental Illness and Co-Occurring Substance Use Disorders," *Behavioral Sciences and the Law,* 2005, vol. 23, pp. 163-170. Also: Pew, "Pew Center on the States - One in 31: The Long Reach of American Corrections," 2009. *https://www.pewtrusts.org/~/media/assets/2009/03/02/pspp_1in31_report_final_web_32609.pdf.* (Viewed July 19, 2024) Also: Lt. Christopher J. Hoina, Ret., Cary, NC Police Department, interview July 1, 2013.

12 K. Imas, "Stopping the Revolving Door," State News, The Council of State Governments 2005. *http://www.csg.org* (Viewed July 2, 2009)

13 R. Honberg & D. Gruttadaro. "Flawed Mental Health Policies and The Tragedy of Criminalization," *Corrections Today,* vol. 67, February 2005.

14 Op. Cit., J. Klopovic, M. Vasu, & D. Yearwood. *Effective Program Practices for At-Risk Youth.* Also: H. Steadman, M. Williams-Deane, J. Morrissey, M. Westcott, S. Salasin, & S. Shapiro, "A SAMHSA Research Initiative Assessing the Effectiveness of Jail Diversion Programs for Mentally Ill Persons," *Psychiatric Services,* Dec. 1999, vol. 50, no. 12.

15 Council of State Governments 2002. For a complete explanation of the Council of State Governments Criminal Justice/Mental Health Consensus Project on Involvement with the Mental Health System, please refer to: *https://csgjusticecenter.org/publications/the-consensus-project-report/* (Viewed July 19, 2024)

16 January 2000, Memphis, TN-Delta Watch: 1700 to 0100: 911 Calls extracted from Vickers 2000; 2100 Call, pp. 1-3.

17 *www.memphispolice.org* (Viewed July 19, 2024)

18 H. Lamb, L. Weinberger, & W. DeCuir. "Police and Mental Health," *Psychiatric Services,* 2002, vol. 53, pp. 1266-1271.

19 Pew, "Pew Center on the States – One in 31: The Long Reach of American Corrections," 2009. *https://www.pewtrusts.org/~/media/assets/2009/03/02/pspp_1in31_report_final_web_32609.pdf.* (Viewed July 19, 2024). Also: Frontline, *The New Asylums,* PBS, 10 May 2005. *http://www.pbs.org/wgbh/pages/frontline/shows/asylums/etc/synopsis.html* (Viewed July 19, 2024) Also: A. Rich, "Mental Illness and the Criminal Justice System," *State Government News,* 2002, *www.csg.org* (Viewed July 2, 2009)

20 B. Vickers, *Memphis Tennessee, Police Department's Crisis Intervention Team,* Bureau of Justice Assistance Clearinghouse, Rockville, MD, 2000, 2315 Call, pp. 1-3.

21 J. Oliva & M. Compton. "A Statewide Crisis Intervention Team (CIT) Initiative: Evolution of the Georgia CIT Program," *J Am Acad Psychiatry Law,* 2008, 36:1:38-46.

22 J. Tremblay, *Towards an Integrated Network: Working Together to Avoid Criminalization of People with Mental Health Problems,* Marquardt Printing Co., Ltd., Ottawa, ON, 2008.

23 Op. Cit., Council of State Governments, Criminal Justice.

24 E. McWilliams, *How to Survive Best Practice,* University of New South Wales Press Ltd., Sydney, NSW, 2002.

25 Op. Cit., Frontline, *The New Asylums,* PBS.

26 M. Gladwell, "Million-Dollar Murray: Why Problems Like Homelessness May Be Easier to Solve Than to Manage," *The New Yorker,* iss. 02-13 and 20, 2006.

27 Op. Cit., Pew, "Pew Center on the States – One in 31," 2009.

28 The Capacity Building Series outlines a comprehensive local reentry strategy for juveniles, adults, and the mentally ill involved with the criminal justice system or at risk of becoming

involved. The book on juvenile reentry considers that the best anti-crime and decriminalization program for children is to successfully and meaningfully keep them in primary and secondary school.

29 Ibid.

30 The LME is the local operational structure of the North Carolina Division of Mental Health, Developmental Disabilities, and Substance Abuse Services. It's responsible for the execution and administration of the Division's policies, procedures, and services.

31 For a good, practical elaboration of what can be done within the criminal justice and mental health systems after arrest, refer to the Council of State Governments 2002 Consensus Project at *https://csgjusticecenter.org/publications/the-consensus-project-report/* (Viewed July 19, 2024). This explains post-booking criminal justice alternatives. There is also the sequential intercept model, which discusses what can be done with the criminal justice system and the community to decriminalize the mentally ill: *www.prainc.com/sim* (Viewed July 19, 2024).

32 E. McWilliams, *How to Survive Best Practice,* University of New South Wales Press Ltd., Sydney, NSW, 2002.

33 H. Macdonald, "A crime theory demolished," *The Wall Street Journal,* 7 Jan. 2010.

34 M. Reuland, L. Draper, & B. Norton. *Improving Responses to People with Mental Illnesses: Tailoring Law Enforcement Initiatives to Individual Jurisdictions,* Council of State Governments Justice Center and the Police Executive Research Forum for the Bureau of Justice Assistance, Office of Justice Programs, U.S. Department of Justice, Washington, DC, 2010.

35 Ibid, pp. 3-5.

36 *http://www.citinternational.org* (Viewed July 19, 2024).

37 A. Cissner & Farole. *"Avoiding Failures of Implementation: Lessons from Process Evaluations,"* Center for Court Innovation and The Bureau of Justice Assistance, Washington, D.C., 2009.

38 Ibid.

39 Ibid.

40 K. Callahan & K. Kloby. "Moving toward outcome-oriented performance measurement systems," Managing for Performance and Results Series, IBM Center for The Business of Government, Washington, DC, 2009.

41 Op. Cit., Reuland, Draper, & Norton, 2010.

42 C. Hoina, "Crisis Intervention Teams (CIT) in North Carolina: A Template for Success," unpublished consulting guide, 2010.

43 Op. Cit., Reuland, Draper, and Norton 2010.

44 Op. Cit., Hoina 2010.

45 Op. Cit., Reuland, Draper & Norton 2010.

46 M. Reuland, *A Guide to Implementing Police-Based Diversion Programs for People with Mental Illness,* Delmar, NY: The TAPA Center for Jail Diversion, 2004.

47 H. Steadman, "Practical Advice on Jail Diversion: Ten Years of Learnings on Jail Diversion from the CMHS National GAINS Center," 2007, p. 28. *http://www.pacenterofexcellence.pitt.edu/documents/PracticalAdviceOnJailDiversion.pdf* (Viewed May 14, 2012)

48 Op. Cit., Reuland 2004.

49 *http://www.parkridge.us/assets/1/Documents/cpsjMentalHealthResourceGuide052016.pdf* (Viewed May 25, 2016)

50 D. Wells & L. Doherty. A Handbook for Strategic Planning, 2010. *http://unpan1.un.org/intradoc/groups/public/documents/aspa/unpan002504.pdf* (Viewed May 14, 2012.)

51 Ibid.

52 Op. Cit., Reuland, Draper, & Norton 2010.

53 Adapted from B. Vickers, Memphis Tennessee, Police Department's Crisis Intervention Team, Bureau of Justice Assistance Clearinghouse, Rockville, MD, 2000.

54 At the time of this writing, the Five County Mental Health Authority operated a superior crisis center in Henderson, North Carolina. (No longer available) The Authority, besides having drop-off capability, assisted individuals and families experiencing a mental illness, developmental disability, or addictive disorder. It supported individuals in accomplishing personal goals, meeting desired life outcomes, and living successfully in the community of their choice. The center achieved this by utilizing many local, high-quality, compassionate providers who tailor services and support to meet the unique needs of those involved.

55 This story was adapted from the following website *https://www.policeone.com/sponsored-article/articles/484237006-Why-a-different-approach-is-needed-when-interacting-with-people-with-disabilities/*(No longer available) introducing the VITALS app, a helpful resource in the diversion process. *https://rapidsos.com/why-the-vitals-app-became-rapidsos-ready/* (Viewed July 19, 2024)

56 J. Tremblay, *Towards an Integrated Network: Working Together to Avoid Criminalization of People with Mental Health Problems,* Marquardt Printing Co., Ltd., Ottawa, ON, 2008.

57 Op. Cit., Reuland 2004.

58 "Blueprint for Success: The Bexar County Model – How to Set up a Jail Diversion Program in Your Community," 2010. *http://www.naco.org/sites/default/files/documents/Jail%20Diversion%20Toolkit.pdf* (Viewed July 18, 2024)

59 Op. Cit., Steadman, "Practical Advice on Jail Diversion," 2007, p. 28. *http://www.pacenterofexcellence.pitt.edu/documents/PracticalAdviceOnJailDiversion.pdf.* (Viewed May 14, 2012)

60 Op. Cit., Reuland, Draper, & Norton, 2010.

61 Op. Cit., introducing the VITALS app (now RapidSOS), a helpful resource in the diversion process. *https://rapidsos.com/why-the-vitals-app-became-rapidsos-ready/* (Viewed July 19, 2024)

62 Op. Cit., Tremblay 2008.

63 *https://mentalhealthrecovery.com/* (Viewed July 18, 2024)

64 *https://www.nami.org/advocacy/policy-priorities/responding-to-crises/psychiatric-advance-directives/*(Viewed July 19, 2024)

65 Op. Cit., The VITALS App.

66 Op. Cit., Reuland, Draper, & Norton 2010.

67 Op. Cit., Hoina 2010.

68 Op. Cit., Steadman 2007.

69 Ibid., p. 48.

70 Ibid.

71 M. Munetz, A. Morrison, J. Krake, B. Young, & M. Woody. "State mental health policy: Statewide implementation of the Crisis Intervention Team program: The Ohio model," *Psychiatric Services,* 2006, vol. 57, pp. 1569-1571.

72 Ibid.

73 Op. Cit., Dupont, Cochran, & Pillsbury, 2007.

74 J. Oliva & M. Compton. "A statewide Crisis Intervention Team (CIT) initiative: Evolution of the Georgia CIT program," *J An Acad Psychiatry Law,* 2008, vol. 36:1, pp. 38-46.

75 Op. Cit., Reuland, Draper, & Norton 2010.

76 Op. Cit., Oliva & Compton 2008.

77 Op. Cit., Reuland 2004.

78 Ibid.

79 Ibid.

80 Op. Cit., Steadman, 2007. This list of resources draws from *Practical Advice on Jail Diversion,* The Center for Mental Health Services, CMHS, National GAINS Center.

www.ingramcontent.com/pod-product-compliance
Lightning Source LLC
Chambersburg PA
CBHW051318020426
42333CB00031B/3396

* 9 7 8 0 9 9 8 2 3 7 2 8 2 *